I REMEMBER WHEN

31 THOUGHTS FOR MIDDLE SCHOOLERS

MARY
DYKSTRA

credo
house publishers

Published in the United States of America by Credo
House Publishers, a division of Credo Communications
LLC, Grand Rapids, Michigan
credohousepublishers.com

ISBN: 978-1-62586-188-7

Cover and interior design by Frank Gutbrod
Editing by Michael A. Vander Klipp

Printed in the United States of America
First edition

INTRODUCTION

I REMEMBER WHEN . . .

MY FAMILY BOUGHT A COTTAGE IN MICHIGAN.

It was a tiny little place on a tiny little lake, and we loved it! The year was 1972 and I was six years old. We were living in Illinois at the time, and all of our relatives lived in Michigan.

We traveled to Michigan often to visit family, but also because my dad was a pastor who preached in a lot of different churches. Having the cottage meant that we could stay there every time we came to Michigan. And bonus—we stayed there all summer! It was Heaven!

I loved everything about the cottage (and still do): I loved the knotty pine walls and big windows looking out to the lake. I loved the small kitchen and old-fashioned pink awnings (which are now long gone). I loved tramping through the woods behind the cottage and, on still mornings, seeing mirror-image reflections of the woods across the lake. I always thought of the cottage as my true home. The other houses we lived in changed with each move we made, but the cottage was the place that we came back to, the place where we made memories. It was home.

This collection of thoughts center around the things I learned during my time spent at our cottage over the years. I hope these stories will inspire you to keep trying, keep learning and to persevere through both the good and the tough times. I hope they help you develop a positive mindset as you learn that your thoughts direct your actions. Mostly, I hope they help you get to know God better. He loves you and has you in the palm of His hand every moment of every day.

1. FAILING, FALLING, AND WINNING

I REMEMBER WHEN . . .

I WATER-SKIED
FOR THE FIRST TIME.

I was about seven or eight years old when I water-skied for the first time!

Everyone water-skied on our lake, except my mom . . . she didn't even like to swim. But everyone else water-skied, and I wanted to learn.

When I started out, I tried to get up on two skis behind our boat but fell every time. I tried behind a friend's boat and fell again. Every time my family went skiing, I tried, fell, swallowed water, tried again, and fell some more, swallowed more water... until I became too tired to keep trying. The next time my family went skiing, I tried again and again, but unfortunately with the same results.

Then one day my neighbor drove his boat over to my house and said, "Let's get you up on skis." I was so excited! He had a completely different way to teach me to ski. Instead of having me start in the water, he told me to sit at the end of the dock with the tips of the skis up. He gave me the rope and said that all I had to do was stand up when the boat pulled me off the dock and he would do the rest.

So I sat there at the end of the dock, life jacket on, rope in place, skis in the water with the tips up. As I watched the boat pull away, the rope got a bit tighter until there was just a little slack left. Then my neighbor pushed the throttle down. The boat sped up, pulling me right up off the dock, and I simply stood up on those skis. It felt so good! After all that time trying, I was really, truly, finally skiing!

It was such an amazing feeling! It felt like I was walking on water! My neighbor and his girlfriend cheered and clapped for me as if I had just won a gold medal in the Olympics. They had been watching me struggle for days, maybe even weeks.

My neighbor's method of teaching me to ski helped me get the hang of what skiing felt like. I was up on skis and skiing! However, I still had to work on getting up out of the water. It was great to ski. It was fun to go in and out of the wake and speed around the tight turns in the coves. But every skier knows that if you can't get up from the water, your ski ride may be short-lived. Skiers who fall need to learn to get back up without a dock to sit on.

So the next time my family went skiing, I once again tried to get up from the water. I tried, tried, and tried some more. I was all ready to go. I had my ski tips out of the water. I had the rope between the tips. I knew I could ski because I had done it before with my neighbor. I watched the rope get tight and yelled, "Hit it!" As the boat picked up speed, I got dragged for a bit and struggled to stand up.

I wobbled around, then the top half of my body got yanked forward, and then I fell face-first into the water. There were other times when my skis slid out in front of me and I fell backwards.

Each time my skis fell off and floated away. I swam over to them and put them back on as the boat swung around. I got everything set to try again. I did this over and over, each time falling and many times getting a mouthful of water. I did this so often, I felt like I swallowed half the lake!

However, I was not about to give up. Everyone on the lake had mastered skiing, and I was going to as well.

I had a good friend, Cheryl, who lived in the cottage right beside me. She, too, wanted to master skiing. We were both the youngest in our families and all our siblings could ski really well, so she and I were determined to learn.

One day we took out her fishing boat, tied a rope to the end of it, and threw out the skis. I jumped into the water, put on the skis, grabbed the rope and told Cheryl to "Hit it." The little fishing boat and its tiny little motor did the trick! The motor had very steady and smooth acceleration, so my arms weren't yanked out of their sockets as the boat sped up, pulling me up with it. Even though the boat was slower, it was strong enough to get me up on skis! I DID IT! I got right up! And it didn't take 1,000 tries!

I skied for a while, and then Cheryl and I switched places. She got in the water while I drove the little boat. She got up on those skis too! After all those many, many tries behind other boats, we both *finally* got up on skis behind a lowly little fishing boat. We were ecstatic!

Now that we understood how it felt to get up on skis from in the water, we could repeat what we needed to do behind bigger boats. We could finally ski! We still had to learn how to slalom, which is skiing on one ski rather than two . . . which we did, but that's a different story.

Learning to ski was hard work; both learning how to actually ski and learning how to get up while in the water. Both parts were difficult and hard to learn, but I finally had learned a skill that I could use for the rest of my life. Just a year or two ago, when I was spending some time at my cottage, that same neighbor who first taught me to ski saw that I was visiting. He drove his boat over to our cottage and I heard him yell, "Hey! Can Mary come out and play?" I laughed and walked out to the end of the dock. He said, "You wanna ski?" and I said, "Yes!"

I hadn't skied for years, but I got right up, kicked off one of the skis, and sailed around the lake, slaloming in and out of the wake and leaving a high spray behind me at each turn. It was exhilarating! If I hadn't put in the work when I was young, I never would have been able to enjoy skiing for the many years that followed.

Today, I see kids try something once or twice and then give up. It boggles my mind. They feel self-conscious and embarrassed when they try and fail. I never once thought about being embarrassed when I was learning how to ski. I'm sure I looked pretty funny falling on my face, and I know people were watching—that's how my neighbor knew I was having a hard time and why he came over to help. But today, it seems like kids are too scared to try anything new; they're too self-conscious, or they somehow think they have to do everything perfectly the first time. And if it doesn't go right the first or second time, they're done.

But seriously, how in the world could anyone be expected to do something perfectly the first time they try it?

I love the saying that goes, "The only time we fail is when we give up trying."

I have enjoyed water-skiing for over 40 years now. If I had given up when I was eight or ten, or even eleven or twelve when I learned to slalom, I would have missed out on year after year of fun times and great memories.

Working hard is rewarding. Mastering a new skill takes a LOT of work, but it pays off in the end. I love this passage from 1 Corinthians 9:24: "Do you not know that in a race all the runners run, but only one gets the prize? Run in such a way as to get the prize." The basic gist of this verse is that all runners who enter a race run, but only one wins. So "run to win."

However, while there were many water-skiing competitions I could have participated in when I was growing up, I never entered one. I did not ski to win; I skied to play. But learning to ski was a HUGE win! I won at learning to ski. I won at learning to get up on skis while in the water. The prize I won for all my hard work was a lifetime of skiing!

Today, I challenge you to win a new skill. What is something you really want to learn to do? Think about the hard work it will take. Realize you *will* mess up, fall, and swallow some water along the way. But if you keep working at it, you will win! While you may not win a competition, or be the best at your new skill, you'll never know what you can do until you try, right? If you enjoy your new activity, if it brings you happiness and a sense of accomplishment, and if you've learned something new that you are proud of, then you win!

 LEARN IT: 1 Corinthians 9:24

 DO IT:
- What skill do you want to learn?
- What steps will you take today to start learning that skill?
- How will you keep trying when you want to give up?

_____

_____

_____

_____

_____

_____

_____

_____

_____

_____

_____

_____

_____

_____

2. STILLNESS AND CANOES

I REMEMBER WHEN . . .

I TOOK A CANOE TRIP
WITH MY DAD.

I was about seven years old and my dad and I had planned a canoe trip to Gun Lake. The little lake we lived on, Payne Lake, was attached to the much larger Gun Lake by a small channel that meandered a mile or so through winding brush and swamp. Going from one lake to the other made for a long canoe ride, especially for a seven-year-old, but I was super excited to go with my dad.

I got up early that day and changed straight from my pjs into my bathing suit. We packed a picnic lunch as well as oodles of bug spray and sunscreen. I got my towel, life jacket, and the canoe paddles. We placed all of our supplies in the middle of the canoe, said a fond farewell to my mother, and started on our big journey to Gun Lake.

I was in the front of the canoe and my dad was steering in the back. We paddled across our lake and came to a low culvert that went under a road. We paddled to the shore, carried the canoe over the road and slid it into the channel. That's when the real journey began.

The channel led through a thick marsh full of birds, fish, and creepy crawly insects. Yet, it was still and quiet (like the water in Psalm 23:2, "He leads me beside quiet waters"). We heard birds chirping and singing. We saw them balancing delicately on reeds that barely bent under their weight. As we'd get close, they'd flit over to a different reed. We heard bullfrogs "garumphing" and turtles flopping into the water, and I watched them swim under the canoe. There were mosquitos, dragonflies, water bugs, deer flies, horse flies—and these bugs loved the marsh and loved circling our heads. I remember the smell and stickiness of the bug spray as I sprayed it all over myself.

Once the bug spray kicked in and the pests left us alone, the marsh was peaceful and quiet. The water was shallow and the channel twisted around sharp curves. When I wasn't helping to paddle, we got stuck in the tall cattails growing along the edge of the channel. My dad grumbled a bit and paddled backwards to get us unstuck, turned the canoe slightly, and got us back on track. Sometimes the water got so shallow we had to scoot our canoe over the sand, shoving at the sand with our paddles as if we were in a gondola.

I remember seeing lily pads with their flowers tightly shut. I remember seeing red-winged blackbirds balancing precariously on reeds or thin branches. I remember seeing herons in the distance, walking gently in the shallows as they looked for their breakfast.

As we got further into the swamp, the sound of the road faded into the distance, and the only sounds we heard were the paddles in the water and the birds, insects, and bullfrogs. I remember imagining what it would have been like to be an explorer or a Native American guide canoeing through the wild in a homemade birch-bark canoe rather than in our lightweight aluminum one.

While my mind was absorbing my surroundings and imagining things that might have happened in the marsh, my dad was just quietly paddling the canoe. We talked a little, but we talked quietly. The thing is, my dad wasn't really a quiet person. He was a very well-known preacher, and when he preached, he was loud! He had a huge presence and people were drawn to God through his preaching. However, here in the canoe, gliding through the marsh, he was mostly quiet.

We did talk about the variety of birds, fish, insects, and plants, noticing different colors of flowers or leaves. Mainly, though, he was quiet, and I was quiet. I imagine that his mind was as full of our surroundings as mine was. We experienced it differently, but we savored it together.

After what seemed like about five hours (but was really only about one), the small stream started to open up and get deeper. The sounds changed as we heard boat motors in the distance, a signal we were getting closer to Gun Lake. We went through a big culvert leading under a bridge—the canoe fit under this one. I always liked going under the bridge because it was cool in the shade and any noise we made echoed and bounced off the metal walls.

Once through the culvert, we went around a bend and the channel got even wider, eventually opening into Gun Lake. We paddled past cottages and headed toward the public beach area.

At this point, the sun was high in the sky and I was getting hot. So I stepped out of the canoe into the shallow water. Gun Lake had a nice sandy bottom, so I dipped into the water to cool off and swam around the canoe. My dad just kept paddling along.

We pulled up to a small opening in the trees near the public beach. We parked the canoe on shore, and I swam some more as my dad sat in the sand. Eventually we unpacked our picnic lunch and ate it together. I played in the water, completely enjoying myself. I think my dad may have taken a nap, or maybe he swam a bit with me. But the thing I remember most was that the whole trip was peaceful and quiet.

To me, these canoe trips were the physical expression of Psalm 46:10: "Be still, and know that I am God." I felt surrounded by God. I felt His presence soak into me as we paddled through the marsh, the beautifully calm surroundings whispering His name. I remember these unique moments, filled with silence and solitude. There was no boredom involved—instead, the solitude was filled with life.

I fully experienced a time to "be still and know that I am God" on those canoe trips. Sometimes in our busy world and in our busy lives, it's hard to stop and be still. Sometimes it's hard to hear God or feel His presence when life is all "go, go, go." But making time to get away and "be still" is well worth the effort.

Are you finding ways that you can be still? Are you finding some beauty in nature and letting God surround you through it? If not, stop what you're doing and look for it. God's beauty is everywhere, and you don't have to be in a canoe to experience it!

"Be still, and know that I am God." Psalm 46:10a

 LEARN IT: Psalm 46:10

 DO IT:
- Write down five places where you see God's beauty. If you can, go to one of these places and sit in silence. Look around. Listen. Be still. Let God's presence surround you.
- Write down what you're feeling and experiencing and savor the moment.

1. the little lake near wes's house
2. Camp chilhaven
3. Camp hume
4. my backyard
5. the mountans

peace, happiness, Quiet

3. STRENGTH AND SAILBOATS ...

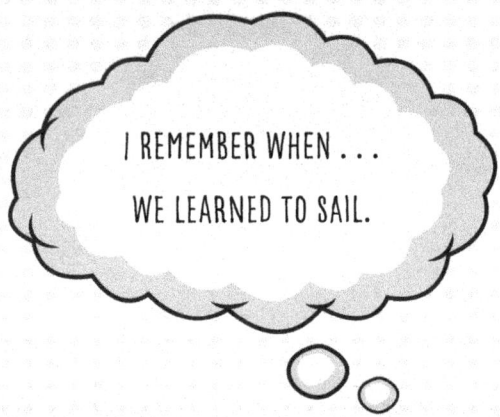

I REMEMBER WHEN ...

WE LEARNED TO SAIL.

A lot of the cottages on the lake had small sailboats. The sails were all similar, with large stripes: blue and white, or yellow and white, or red and white. Ours was light-blue and white. It was always fun to see these little boats gliding back and forth across the lake on a breezy day.

Now that we had a sailboat, I wanted to learn to sail, but of course it wasn't as easy as it looked. Sailboats have a lot of moving parts that all have to be managed at the same time—talk about multi-tasking!

Our boat had a shallow hull with a ten-inch-deep gully in it. There was a slot toward the front of the boat for the keel and a hole beyond that for the mast—the pole that held the sail. The sail attached to the mast, then also to another pole—called the boom—that went straight across the length of the boat. We lifted the sail into place by ropes and it looked like a fluttering, happy striped triangle.

The rudder was at the back of the boat. The sail, the keel, and the rudder were all moving parts that I had to manage to successfully sail the little boat. And, similar to my waterskiing attempts, I didn't always get it right. In fact, I failed many times at sailing. But I didn't let that stop me!

Ha

My dad took me out to teach me the basics. He told me it was pretty easy. I just had to slide the boat out into the lake, drop the keel in the slot when the water got a bit deeper, then hang on to the rope and the rudder, catch the wind, and keep the rudder in a place to angle the boat in such a way as to keep the wind in the sail. Easy peasy.

Yeah right! It was easy for him because he understood all the ins and outs of sailing. The boat had no steering wheel, no motor, and no paddles or oars! It was tricky. At first, I held the rope that pulled the sail while he steered with the rudder. If I pulled hard on the rope, the sail caught the wind, and the boat went faster, zipping across the lake. If I released the sail a bit, we slowed down. Sometimes, if I pulled too hard, the sail lost the wind, so I'd let it out a bit. And sometimes the wind was moving in a funky direction, so I let the sail out more to catch wind. It was always a balancing act, knowing just where the sail needed to be to catch the optimal amount of wind to keep the boat moving.

My friend Cheryl also had a small sailboat. Theirs had a red and white sail. Her dad loved to sail and taught Cheryl while my dad taught me.

Eventually, Cheryl and I decided we knew enough to try sailing on our own. Again, sailing was easy peasy right? Well, I don't know if I'd say it was easy peasy, but we had fun learning and failing in our attempts to sail. Our dads were good at sailing but Cheryl and I somehow managed to tip the boat over as soon as we got into the middle of the lake.

When the breeze was strong, we pulled the boom in so that the sail was full of wind, and we went so fast that the boat was nearly standing on its side as we raced across the water. As inexperienced as we were, sometimes we lost control of the rudder and the boat tipped over, the sail landing flat on the surface of the lake. There were times when the boat tipped all the way over with the bottom of the boat facing the sky and the sail completely submerged. It was a bit more challenging to get it right-side up when that happened, but the boats are very lightweight, so we managed. We swam to one side of the hull and pulled on it until the sail popped back up out of the water. Then we climbed back into the boat, and took off again.

Eventually, we managed to sail across the lake. When we got close to the shore, we had to do a quick turn, especially when we were sailing at a good clip. We pushed the rudder way to the right and quickly ducked under the boom as it swung around. Then we scrambled to the other side of the boat and caught the wind to sail back across the lake.

Easy peasy, right? Not so much. Sometimes one of us got hit by the boom. Sometimes a gust of wind caught the sail while we were trying to turn and tipped the boat over. And sometimes the wind stalled, leaving us sitting in the middle of the lake—slack sail, no oar, no motor, no movement.

During those times, we did what we could to make it back to shore. We paddled with our hands, or moved the rudder back and forth using it as an oar. We tried everything to move just enough, hoping to catch a whisper of a breeze so we could sail again. Sometimes one of our neighbors saw us sitting in the middle of the lake and came out to help. They gave us a rope and a tow back to shore. If we were close enough, we just jumped into the water and swam the boat back to shore.

Sailing was an adventure, and the wind was always the trickiest part. Payne Lake is shaped like a boomerang. Right at the bend (we called it the "point"), the wind always moved in different directions, called crosswinds, and we could never figure out how to catch the wind in a way that would help us get beyond the point to the other section of the lake. We could control the rudder, the keel, and the sail, but we couldn't control the wind! We had to respond to the wind and work with it in order to move the boat.

The same kinds of things happen in life. There are things that are within our control, and there are things that we don't control. No matter what happens, however, we need to keep moving forward.

A pandemic hits. Someone gets cancer. A friend betrays our trust. The wind dies down. The wind picks up. How do we keep our boats on course? How do we keep sailing? How do we keep enjoying the ride?

Sailboats are built to be resilient. The sail cloth is a specific cloth that can get wet and dry quickly. It is lightweight but incredibly strong. Sailboats are lightweight as well and shaped to glide in the water. We're a bit like those boats in that our resilience is what makes us strong. It allows us to respond to shifting winds. It helps us get our boats back up once they tip over. It gets us through crosswinds when we don't know which way to turn. It gets us back to shore when the wind is gone.

So, how can we learn to strengthen our resilience?

Joshua 1:9 is a great passage to memorize and remember when we need to build up our resilience: "Have I not commanded you? Be strong and courageous. Do not be afraid; do not be discouraged, for the LORD your God will be with you wherever you go." In just a few short words, this verse gives us some really great instructions:

Be strong: Sail together! Share your skills with someone else, and learn from them as well as you move across the water of your life.

Be courageous: Respond to the changing winds and the changing circumstances in your life, but keep moving forward.

Remember, God is with you wherever you go: Stay close to the One who calms the waves and the sea, who knows where you need to go, and how to get you safely there.

Those are great words to live by—easy peasy right? Maybe not, but nothing that's really fun or adventurous ever is.

word.

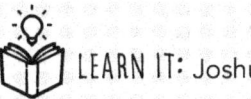 **LEARN IT:** Joshua 1:9

 DO IT:
- Write down a time when you tried something new but stopped when it got too hard.
- Write down a time when you tried something new and kept going until you learned a new skill.
- What steps did you take to learn your new skill?
- Who is someone you admire who has a skill you would love to have? How do they keep learning and refining their skill? What can you learn from them?

①. Shooting

②. piano, theater

③ kept practicing

④ mary buller — mentoring — she just keeps doing it.

4. MUCK AND SAND

I REMEMBER WHEN . . .

WE SWAM AT
THE "SWIMMING HOLE."

When we were kids, we loved swimming up at the "swimming hole."

The water in front of our cottages was great for swimming as long as we didn't touch the bottom. For the most part, the bottom of our lake was muck! As kids, it didn't bother us too much because we were used to it. At the ends of the docks where we started skiing, the speedboats always churned up the ground and for some reason this helped pack the muck into a harder surface. But if we went into the lake from the shore, we sank into the muck up to our ankles. It was oozy and squishy. The water got all cloudy and we couldn't see the bottom. Sometimes we even hit a sinkhole, and sink into muck up to our knees!

I remember using an inflatable raft as one way to avoid the muck. I started on shore where it was sandy, walked a couple of steps into the water, put the raft in, did a belly flop on it, and glided into deeper water. This way I didn't have to walk in the muck or touch the seaweed.

But the swimming hole was different. It had a wonderful sandy bottom all the way out to the floating dock. There were no sinkholes, no muck, and no seaweed. The floating dock was about 50 feet out and it was tied to big posts that were driven into the ground. During the fall, when we took the floating dock out of the lake for the winter, we tied plastic milk jugs to the posts to show us where to attach the dock again in the spring. They also signaled visiting boaters and fishermen to steer clear of the unseen posts.

But in the summer, it was our gathering place. Everyone from our landing and from the point went to the swimming hole.

During the weekday mornings, when a lot of the families were at work, Cheryl and I spent hours at the swimming hole, pretending we were mermaids, or playing with our canoe, or making our wet hair look like George Washington's. We loved being in the water. We ran down the hill right into the lake, diving under and making a huge splash. We never walked slowly into the water; we always went in with a running dive. That's how all the kids went into the swimming hole; run down the hill, throw a towel on the railing or grass, run into the water and dive, slapping the water and splashing it high.

In the afternoons, things started to pick up. First, around 2:00-ish, the moms gathered, leaving their cottages and coming together to take a dip and cool off before they went back to start making dinner. Next, maybe around 4:00-ish, the older kids who had summer jobs returned back from work.

Then, a game of keep-away started, full of chucking tennis balls and water-tackling anyone and everyone. I remember when the ball came out of someone's hand and floated free in the water for a short time. Those nearby splashed their way over trying to grab it. People slapped the water around the ball, splashing and making waves so no one could even see where the ball was. As soon as someone grabbed for it, others splashed again, trying to get the ball away from the opposing team. It was mayhem, and it was fun, and the games lasted for hours.

On Saturdays or holidays, it'd be so busy sometimes we just swam in front of our cottages because there were just too many people at the swimming hole. Wherever we chose to swim, we were always aware of the ground: muck or sand; sink in ooze or walk on top of hard ground. The contrast was huge.

It reminds me of the famous Bible passage about building a house on rock or sand. I even remember a childhood song about this passage, motions and all.

The foolish man built his house upon the sand
The foolish man built his house upon the sand
The foolish man built his house upon the sand
And the rains came tumbling down.
The rains came down and the floods came up
The rains came down and the floods came up
The rains came down and the floods came up
And the house on the sand when SPLAT!

The wise man built his house upon the rock
The wise man built his house upon the rock
The wise man built his house upon the rock
And the rains came tumbling down.
The rains came down and the floods came up
The rains came down and the floods came up
The rains came down and the floods came up
And the house on the rock stood firm.

So build your house on the Lord Jesus Christ
So build your house on the Lord Jesus Christ
So build your house on the Lord Jesus Christ
And the blessings will come down
The blessings will come down as the prayers go up
The blessings will come down as the prayers go up
The blessings will come down as the prayers go up
So build your house on the Lord.

If we sang this song about the ground in Payne Lake, the foolish man would build on muck because that was the unstable foundation; the sand in the lake was firm. Either way, the message is pretty much the same.

When we build our lives, do we want to stand on muck (or even sand that shifts and moves when we walk on it), or do we want to stand on rock, which is solid and reliable? I know that when life around me is shifting, moving, and I feel like I may be sinking, I want something solid to hold on to. That solid thing is God and my faith in Him.

Even when my faith isn't too strong, it still has the rock-solid foundation that God is who He says He is. This is something I have never doubted. I've doubted and questioned how things work, why bad things happen, and why I feel like some of my prayers don't get answered or are answered differently than what I've prayed for. But the thing that remains solid through all of this is God, and the fact that He listens to me, loves me, and gave His Son for me (and you).

That is the rock-solid foundation that has never shifted or moved. It is so solid that all my questions and doubts can sit on that foundation, and it still doesn't move. In fact, this foundation helps me put my questions and doubts and fears into places where I can figure some of them out and accept the ones I can't figure out. And for those ones that simply don't have answers, the foundation is so strong that I can leave those with God, knowing He's got it all in the palm of His hand.

What are you standing on? Is the foundation of your life firm, or do you feel it shifting?

 LEARN IT: Matthew 7:24–27

 DO IT:
- How do you react when your emotions seem to take over and things get crazy?
- What are some things that make you feel like you're sinking? What are some things you can do to stand on a firm foundation?
- How can God be a foundation for your life?

1) typically I cry or need to take Deep breaths

2) multipal people critizizing me at once.
  • Breath

3) asking god for Comfort, & Peace 3 wisdom

5. CANOES AND CREATIVITY

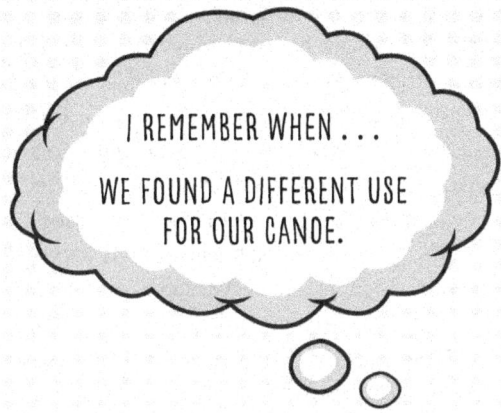

I REMEMBER WHEN . . .

WE FOUND A DIFFERENT USE FOR OUR CANOE.

I loved our canoe. It was silver, lightweight, and could easily glide through the water. It was great because Cheryl and I could be so quiet in the canoe. We paddled around trying not to make a sound. I remember pretending to be Sacagawea, paddling as quietly as I could so as not to disturb any birds, bugs, turtles or fish.

We canoed over to the other side of the lake past the woods. The lake was like glass as we paddled along the shore. It was quiet and still. We could smell the leaves and the wildflowers and see our reflection in the water.

On that side of the lake, there were trees that had fallen down and lay in the water, stretched out from the shore. These logs were the perfect spot for the turtles to sit and soak in the sun. We paddled along and got as close as we could to the "turtle logs." We gently dipped our paddles into the water, easing the canoe forward, and then gliding along without using our paddles to see how close we could get to them. As soon as we got too close, one or two turtles would flop into the water. We watched them swim under the canoe. Others followed their lead, flopped into the water and swam away. The medium-sized turtles were the first to go, followed by the little baby turtles. The big old turtles weren't terribly threatened by two girls in a canoe. They hung out on the log until we got really close. Eventually, they too, flopped into the water, seemingly annoyed by these two young girls disturbing their time in the sun.

I loved watching the turtles. They hung out on a couple of different logs. Once we passed the first log, we headed down to the next log. This one was close to the channel to Gun Lake, and there were so many turtles on this one that it was like the "swimming hole" for the turtles of Payne Lake! But they too plopped into the water as our canoe drew near.

On the opposite side of the lake, on the other end of the boomerang, was a channel to Mud Lake. Cheryl and I loved taking the canoe to Mud Lake too. This was much easier, as the channel was shorter than the one that led to Gun Lake. We could paddle the canoe through a big culvert. It went under the road and was always filled with cobwebs and surrounded by lily pads. I loved hearing our voices and the gentle sound of our oars in the water echo off the sides of the culvert. Sometimes we put our paddles in the canoe, grabbed hold of the top of the culvert, and flung the canoe forward. Once we were out of the culvert, it was just a short paddle through the reeds and lily pads to get to Mud Lake. Mud Lake was very small with no houses on it. It had a public boat ramp for those who wanted to go fishing, and there was a YMCA outdoor camp across the lake.

The other place we liked to take the canoe was to the swimming hole. This is where we used the canoe differently from its intended purpose. Canoes, like sailboats, can tip over rather easily. We didn't tip the canoe by accident—we did it for fun.

When we got to the swimming hole, we put all our gear on the shore, then walked the canoe into water that was about waist deep. My sister joined us as we tipped the side of the canoe into the water and watched the water flow in. One of us climbed in and sat in the middle on the floor, holding the bar that spanned across the canoe, kind of like a seat in a roller coaster. Once filled, the canoe sat low in the water, with only about two to three inches of silver still above the water. Those of us outside of the canoe grabbed hold of the edges and flipped it over, spinning it through the water. The person sitting in the canoe held her breath, was plunged into the water, swept upside-down through the water, and came up on the other side. It was a blast! We spun the canoe as fast as we could and we took turns sitting in the canoe and spinning around. It was fun when we got good at spinning. The person in the canoe would be spun through the water, come out, take a deep breath and be plunged back into the water to spin once again, sometimes going round three, four, even five times in a row.

When people came to visit, we spun them in the canoe, and when I had kids of my own, I taught them how to do it. They too loved it! It was like a homemade water park ride!

We loved using the canoe differently from its intended purpose. It was creative and unique. I love it when people come up with new ways to use everyday items—like binder clips! Have you ever seen any of those online videos that show all the ways to use a binder clip? Or those food or fashion challenges where they take everyday objects and repurpose them? Maybe you've done this at home or at school? Repurposing items can be fun and it takes an imaginative mind to think outside the box.

In working with kids over the years, I've heard so many of them say, "I'm not creative" or "I'm not good at art." But the thing is EVERY one of us is created in God's image. Genesis 1:27 tells us; "So God created mankind in his own image, in the image of God he created them; male and female he created them." That's only one of many Bible passages that refer to humans being created in God's image.

So what does this have to do with being creative? Well, let's look at the very first verse in the Bible, Genesis 1:1:

"In the beginning God created . . ."

The very first words of the Bible talk about God creating. He made the world, stars, planets, sun and moon, animals, people, plants, air, and everything else that's ever been created. He made everything. And we, you and I, are created in HIS image. GOD CREATED—We are made in His image—WE CREATE. It's how we've been made. It's a part of every one of us. The problem comes when we choose to ignore our creativity, decide that our creative efforts aren't good enough, or dismiss creativity, thinking it's not as valuable as other ways of thinking or working.

However, being creative doesn't have to be complex or difficult! It can be as easy as spinning a canoe—that is being creative! Adding pesto to grilled cheese shows creativity! Rearranging your bedroom is being creative! Being created in God's image means that we too create.

Creativity is built into who we are, and it can be seen in ways that go far beyond drawing a sketch or painting a picture. So, how are you being creative today? How are you living out being "created in God's image"? Love to hear about it!

 LEARN IT: Genesis 1:1

 DO IT:
- Find an everyday object. Try a bunch of different things with the object and discover a new use for it.
- Describe how you used the object in a whole new way.
- Share your new idea with someone!

_____
_____
_____
_____
_____
_____
_____
_____
_____

6. LAKES, SILVER, AND MIRROR REFLECTIONS

I REMEMBER WHEN . . .

THE LAKE LOOKED LIKE GLASS.

Early in the morning, the reflection of the woods stretched almost all the way across the lake. It was beautiful. The reflection was so clear, a mirror image of the trees and sky. On really still mornings, it could be an hour or two before there was even a ripple on the water. Sometimes a breeze floated across the lake, making small, tiny waves, and soon enough, water smoothed out to glass once again.

Whippoorwills called and various other birds sang, and sometimes I heard their wings flapping in the air. I loved watching the herons and sand cranes walk stealthily in the water, not making a sound—these big, beautiful birds walking on stick legs, gracefully and slowly stepping through the shallows. They were so poised that they barely made a ripple.

I loved the lake when it looked like this. Every now and then a fishing boat glided by. I heard a line cast out and the small "plop" of the baited hook landing on the water. I heard a click and the tick of the gears as the person fishing started reeling in the line. I remember seeing fish jump and hearing them splash into the water. I watched as the ring they left expanded and eventually dissipated until the water was still once again. I could sit for hours just looking at the lake.

When I had kids of my own, my dad bought me a paddleboard. I loved taking the paddleboard out on still mornings. I glided along on the water, trying not to break the "glass." I took the board all the way around the lake. Our side of the boomerang was always much more still than the other side. When I passed the swimming hole, there was always a breeze making small ripples in the water. I paddled along, looking at the cottages, passing some fishing boats and waving to neighbors, who also loved quiet mornings. I paddled past the channel to Mud Lake and along the stretch of cottages of people we didn't know. I paddled into Hoving's cove and past the boat launch. It wasn't until I got back to our side of the boomerang, across from the cottage along the woods by the turtle logs, that the water was once again like glass.

I loved watching the paddleboard cut through the water. I glided, almost silently, making my own tiny waves. The turtles weren't on the logs yet, as the logs were still in the shade, but quiet morning sounds filled the woods: a flap of wings here, a rustle in the trees there. I looked down and saw fish swimming under the paddleboard. The lily pad flowers were tightly closed. Dragonflies flitted from lily pad to lily pad, landing silently.

I kept paddling past the channel to Gun Lake, and around the bend to the stretch of water leading back to our own little cottage. I pushed the paddleboard on shore and stepped into the water. More neighbors were awake and on their decks with their morning coffee. We greeted each other then lapsed back into silence, savoring the still morning.

The reflection of the trees and sky was so clear. It reminded me of things I learned about reflecting Christ. Growing up, through school, church, and youth group, I was taught to be Christ's hands and feet, to "reflect" Him to everyone I met. This is part of being created in His image. When we're created in someone's image, we reflect that image to others around us. Think of how kids look like their parents—they are literally made in their parents' image! And as we are made in God's image, we are encouraged, or "called," to reflect Him, like a lake reflects the trees.

I remember reading an article about Malachi 3:3, a passage that talks about how God refines us. It says, "He will sit as a refiner and purifier of silver; he will purify the Levites and refine them like gold and silver." The article told a story about a woman visiting a silversmith. This story really helped me understand on a deeper level how the process of refining silver relates to being a reflection of Christ. No one seems to know where the story originated, but it goes like this:

> As she watched the silversmith, he held a piece of silver over the fire in a metal cup held by a long set of tongs and let it heat up. He explained that in refining silver, one needed to hold the silver in the middle of the fire where the flames were hottest so as to burn away all the impurities. The woman thought about God holding us in such a hot spot; then she thought again about the verse that says, "He will sit as a refiner

and purifier of silver" (Malachi 3:3). She asked the silversmith if it was true that he had to sit there in front of the fire the whole time the silver was being refined. The man answered that yes, he not only had to sit there holding the silver, but he had to keep his eyes on the silver the entire time it was in the fire. If the silver was left a moment too long in the flames, it would be destroyed. The woman was silent for a moment. Then she asked the silversmith, "How do you know when the silver is fully refined?" He smiled at her and answered, "Oh, that's easy—when I see my image in it."

This story opened my eyes to a new understanding of being a reflection of Christ. It helped me see that He wants to get rid of the things in me that don't reflect who He is. When people look at me, He wants them to see Him without me having to yell, "I'M A CHRISTIAN!" When I truly reflect Christ, people should see Him in my demeanor, my character, in the decisions I make, and in the way I treat others—they should see in all my character traits that I love the Lord.

When I taught in a public school, I couldn't talk about my faith. I couldn't put Bible verses on the board, pray with my students, or point to God as the greatest Artist. However, I tried to reflect Christ to my students. I prayed for my students every day, and I silently prayed for them as we sat in class.

I remember one student came up to me, and asked, "You're a Christian aren't you?" I couldn't tell if he was accusing me, or just making a statement, but I cautiously answered, "Yes, I am." I pressed him a bit on why he asked, and he said, "I can just tell. You're different." I must say it was one of the highest compliments I've ever received.

Reflection is a pretty amazing thing. Whether it's a completely still lake reflecting trees and sky and clouds, a mirror that we use daily, or godly characteristics that help us stand apart from others, the concept of reflection is a bit mysterious. We take it for granted without really thinking about it. The science behind it is something I don't fully understand. All I know is that it's pretty cool.

I remember looking at the lake and just watching to see when it would change. Would a breeze pick up and break the reflection? Would a boat go past? How long would people wait to go out on the water?

And what about us? Do we always reflect Christ, or are there things that come along and disturb that reflection? How can we check our lives to make sure we are reflecting Christ? It's mysterious, but if we stay close to Him through our daily spiritual habits, and then put those habits into our lives and have character that is "refined by fire," the reflection will be that of Christ.

When you see a reflection today, either through a mirror, on the water, or even in a spoon, think about how you are a reflection of Christ. Then ask Him to use your reflection today to be a blessing to someone else.

LEARN IT: Malachi 3:3

DO IT:

- Choose three friends and write down one adjective they would use to describe you.
- Think about those three words. Are they characteristics that reflect God?
- How can you use one of those characteristics today and make someone else's day better?

_____

_____

_____

_____

_____

_____

_____

_____

_____

_____

_____

_____

_____

_____

_____

_____

7. FRIED FISH AND GOD'S LOVE

I REMEMBER WHEN . . .

WE HAD A FISH FRY.

My dad was an avid fisherman, and his greatest joy in life, besides preaching, was fishing. He loved to fish, and went every chance he got. He had a small fishing boat that he took out early in the mornings or later in the evenings. My brothers and sister loved fishing with him. Sometimes my mom fished with him. He had friends who fished with him as well. He fished on our lake and all the little lakes surrounding ours. He loved to fish!

He also kept all the fish he caught (if they were big enough) so that we could eat them. He had a table set up outside by the garage where he cleaned the fish while Cheryl and I watched. He had a system and could do it as fast as lightning. He chopped off the head, slit the belly, pulled out the guts, sliced the fish in half, then trimmed the bones and peeled off the skin. Enthralled and completely grossed out by the whole process, Cheryl and I loved watching him clean the fish. There was something fascinating about it all. It was slimy, smelly, and bloody, and all the gory things drew our attention.

Every time he went out fishing and came back with a haul, he cleaned the fish, bagged them up, and then put them in the freezer. Once we had a big stash, we had a fish fry. We put the frozen fish into the sink to thaw, and then a completely new process began. My dad set up a fry pan outside so that the cottage wouldn't smell like fish. He had a crumb mix of some sort, and he changed it as he tried different techniques. The fish were small pieces, and he could fit about 10–12 in the frying pan at one time. He fried them, then put them in a 9x13 pan that Cheryl and I transferred into the kitchen to be put in the oven to stay warm. During the short distance from the backyard to the kitchen, Cheryl and I snuck one or two pieces of fish and ate them!

We LOVED the fried fish. I remember when all the fish were fried and it was time for supper, Cheryl stood in the kitchen (just about a foot taller than the counter), looking longingly at the fish, wanting so badly to stay and eat supper with us. On her way out the door, she whispered to me, "Save me some of the fish." So I did.

Before we sat down to supper, I grabbed a small paper bag. As we ate supper, I put the paper bag in my lap, ready to smuggle some of the fish into the bag. I was so sneaky. I ate a fish and put a fish into the bag. I ate another one and slipped another one into the bag. I kept this up, asking for second and third helpings until me, and the bag, were nice and full. As the youngest child, no one paid that much attention to me, so I filled up the bag without anyone knowing. After we cleaned up from supper, I went next door with the bag of fish. We sat on Cheryl's bed and I watched her eat all of the fish in the bag!

Now when we talk about it, we laugh, recalling our sneaky ways. Every single time we had fish (and we had fish a lot), she asked me to sneak a bunch for her. One day my mom noticed and asked, "What are you doing?" I said, "I'm saving some of the fish for Cheryl. She loves it and wants me to save some for her." My parents thought this was hilarious. Being extremely generous people, they gladly set aside some fish for her. Then we just invited her to stay for supper and when she did, she packed away more fish than any of us. If she couldn't stay, we set a paper bag on the counter and loaded it up with fish just for Cheryl to have whenever she wanted.

Cheryl loved fish. I loved fish. I could have it whenever I wanted, but Cheryl's family didn't make fish like my dad did. I had something she wanted and loved.

The fried fish remind me of God's love and how some people don't know about it. Just like our family had fish to share, our family also knew God's love. Those of us who know and love Jesus have something to share with others.

Growing up, my dad preached all over the country and the world. We traveled a lot with him and when I was a teenager, I went with him to India. Back then, people in India and China and other places had a harder time finding out about Jesus and His love. My dad did a lot of work telling people about Jesus and salvation. In a sense, he had to sneak "paper bags full of fish" into these countries to share the story of God's love.

Many people in the world want to know more about Christianity. The problem is they may not have a Bible in their language or a Christian church nearby. They may not have any way to get any more information about Jesus and His gift of salvation. Growing up, because of my dad's work,

I was very aware of other people groups around the world and passages like Mark 16:15 that tell us to "Go into all the world and preach the gospel to all creation."

My dad took this passage literally—it's what he did for a living. In addition to preaching and traveling, he devoted much of his time to his work in India, writing Bible studies and kids' workbooks so that people could learn about salvation. He set up an organization that helped people learn how to read and taught them about the Lord. This organization also helped train Indian people to be pastors and start their own churches. They helped women learn to read and improve their lives. He also smuggled Bibles into China when he traveled because at that time in China it was against the law to have a Bible.

Just as I smuggled that crispy-fried fish to Cheryl, my dad brought the good news about Jesus around the world. It wasn't against the law for me to smuggle the fish, but Cheryl didn't have any, and I had it in abundance.

In the same way, God's word and His love are abundant. John 10 tells how Jesus came to share His love with people. I love verse 10, where it says: "I came that you may have life and have it abundantly."

God's love is for us to share as freely as my family shared the fish with Cheryl. It's for us to share as freely as giving a smile to someone who's having a bad day. It's for us to share by giving some of our money to organizations like the one my dad set up (now called Mission India) and the many other organizations that use the money well and bring God's love to people around the world. It's for us to share by helping out at a soup kitchen, or in our own churches and communities. The ways we can share God's love are endless.

Life with God is abundant! His love is abundant. How can you share that with someone today?

 LEARN IT: Mark 16:15

 DO IT:
- How can you share God's love with someone today?
- Is there an organization either locally or around the world that you'd like to support?
- Can you share God's love with a friend?
- What are some ways you can share God's love?

_____

_____

_____

_____

_____

_____

_____

_____

_____

8. SHUFFLING CARDS AND RAINY DAYS

I REMEMBER WHEN . . .
IT RAINED AT THE COTTAGE.

It didn't seem to happen that often, and usually lasted only a day or two, and Cheryl and I didn't mind rainy days too much. In fact, a rainy day provided a fun change of pace. It didn't stop us from playing in the water, unless there was thunder or lightning. If we heard thunder, we jumped out of the water, grabbed our towels, and headed into one of our cottages. Sometimes, we sat on our towels on the floor and just watched TV. But usually we did something else.

Cheryl's grandma had a cottage up on the hill by the swimming hole. All the adults called Cheryl's grandma by her nickname: "Babe." I always thought it was a funny nickname because she looked very much like a grandma, and not like a "Babe." She was a funny lady though; when she got frustrated with Cheryl, she called her "fart blossom."

Cheryl and I loved going to her grandma's cottage, and it was especially fun on rainy days because Babe loved playing cards. Playing cards was a big thing out at the cottage. All the adults played together, our older siblings played, and Cheryl's grandma even played alone—game after game of solitaire. On rainy days, we could spend the whole day playing cards with her grandma. I remember watching Babe shuffle the cards. She was a master at shuffling. Her shuffling was so cool that on one rainy day, we asked her to teach us how to shuffle, and of course, she did.

She had at least 20 decks of cards (probably more) at her cottage. I remember having to count the cards in each deck before we began playing an actual game to make sure we had a full deck. Some games required that each of us have our own deck of cards, so we shuffled each deck to start a new hand. Her shuffling was an art! It was similar to the card sharks you see on TV who deal for international poker challenges. As we watched, the cards flew through her hands in a bunch of different ways, bending this way and then that way, sliding together, making a bridge and then starting all over again. Each shuffle was a three-step process, which we repeated numerous times to make sure the cards were mixed well. If they weren't, the cards could give an unfair advantage to any given player. If that happened, we heard about it throughout the whole game: "No fair! Did you even shuffle those cards? Redo!" and on and on it went.

On this rainy day, she agreed to teach us how to shuffle, so we sat down at her wooden, oval dining table right by her kitchen with Babe at the head. It was strange having only three people at that big table. Normally, Babe and Cheryl's whole family, including their friends and girlfriends or boyfriends, were around that table. But on this day, it was just the three of us. I remember watching Babe's weathered hands flipping through the cards. I remember her gray curls, blue eyes, and quick wit; ready to call Cheryl a "fart blossom" as soon as she felt it was necessary.

Shuffling cards was serious business. Cheryl sat on one side of Babe and I sat on the other. We each had a deck of cards in our hands, and Babe demonstrated. Splitting the deck in half was the first step. Most people I knew simply put the deck on the table and took off the top half, but that wasn't how Babe did it. She took the whole deck in her right hand and skillfully split in two. As she bent the deck, the cards flipped through her fingers until half of the deck separated from the other half. With her left hand, she slid the separated half around, never dropping a card, so that she had half of the deck in each hand. She was fast as lightning. It only took her a second to split the deck in two.

Next, she held each half the same way, thumb at the top, pointer finger curled up in the middle and her pinky at the bottom. She bent the cards inward, bringing the two sides together at the top. She then let the tips of each deck flip through her thumbs and the two halves slid into each other. Once the tips of the two halves combined, her hands shifted a bit, cradling the cards and pushing the deck into a "bridge." The cards flew through the bridge and all fell into place, stacked neatly on top of one another.

This whole process only took a few seconds! She did it so fast, the cards flew through each other and got neatly rearranged so we could play a new game. It was a great thing to learn, and I've shuffled in this "fancy" way ever since that day. Once we learned how to shuffle, we moved up a notch in the "kid" category from "little kid who's slow and can't shuffle" to "kid who learned how to shuffle and now has some value" category. Now when we played cards with the big kids, they didn't grab the deck out of our hands; they saw that we had the skills to shuffle when it was our turn. Of course, we didn't master this skill overnight. On rainy days, Cheryl and I each sat with a deck of cards and practiced our technique so we could be as good as Babe.

While some people look at rainy summer days as a downer, Cheryl and I always found different ways to have fun. Rain happens. And, just like everything in life, our perspective can change how we view a rainy day. Either we can see it as an opportunity to get creative, or we can get mad that we can't do the things we love to do. The point is, the rain won't last. The sun will shine again and life without rain will continue.

Sometimes we get frustrated with our circumstances, and even though we know that our frustration doesn't change circumstances that are completely out of our control (like a rainy day or a worldwide pandemic), the frustration is still there.

If you're currently "stuck" and frustrated, I challenge you to consider a change in perspective. Even if you're not stuck now, remember this when you do get stuck (because we all get stuck at some point). When things are out of your control, how can you view the circumstances as an opportunity to change your perspective? Here's a passage from James 1:2–4 that encourages us:

"Consider it pure joy, my brothers and sisters, whenever you face trials of many kinds, because you know that the testing of your faith produces perseverance. Let perseverance finish its work so that you may be mature and complete, not lacking anything."

I know that learning how to shuffle cards on a rainy day is not the kind of "trial" referred to in this passage. But it is referring to the *mindset* we have when we face an obstacle. So let's think about this. Life at the cottage was an outside life. We played in the water, took out the boats, ran around outside, and rode our bikes. We played whiffle ball and "kick the can." We were always outside, from dawn to dusk. But on rainy days, our everyday lives changed. Our lives as we knew them changed.

Rainy days can happen in a lot of ways: whether it's a pandemic that suddenly changes our everyday routines, a bad grade, moving to a new house or state, sickness, a broken bone—you name it, "rainy days" happen. So this verse from James helps us think about our mindset. Are we complaining when something goes wrong or happens differently from what we expected? Or are we embracing the opportunity to learn, to struggle, and to persevere?

This passage from James 1 encourages us to have a mindset that doesn't mope around when things aren't going our way. It encourages us to refrain from complaining, and to find something joyful about those rainy days, and in "rainy-day" times in our lives.

Rainy days can be trying, both literally and figuratively. But if we embrace the challenge of the rain, it can be an opportunity for us to learn something new.

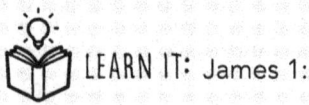 **LEARN IT:** James 1:2–4

 DO IT:
- What trials are you facing today?
- How can you look at these trials as opportunities?
- Write down a life situation that you find challenging, and then think about and write down how that situation can also be an opportunity for you to change your perspective and learn something new.

_____

_____

_____

_____

_____

_____

_____

_____

_____

_____

_____

_____

_____

_____

_____

_____

_____

9. CHARACTER AND CLOTHING

I REMEMBER WHEN . . .

CHERYL AND I HAD
A FASHION SHOW.

One day while we were at her cottage, Cheryl found a big box filled with bathing suits. We opened the box, pulled out each item, examined it and laughed at the variety! These bathing suits were from her older sisters, her mom and her grandma, Babe. They were so funny, we decided to have a fashion show and model each one.

We got our moms together and had them sit in lawn chairs in the yard. We started with the "mom" suits: one-piece bathing suits that hung on our small bodies, with large pointy cups that our preteen bodies didn't fill. Our moms laughed and clapped for us as we sauntered outside in the oversized suits, strutting down our grassy "catwalk." We posed, turned, and posed again before we fell into a fit of giggles and ran back into her cottage for the next round.

The next round was bikinis. Cheryl had two sisters who were much older, so we put on their bikinis. They were still too big for us, but they were way cooler than the "mom" suits. I remember one of them was white crocheted material with beige lining. It was the ultimate cool bikini. I remember her oldest sister wore it all the time and it fit her perfectly. We put on the suits and again sauntered out, cat walking in front of our moms, and they dutifully clapped once more.

The last round was the funniest of all as we put on her Grandma Babe's suits. These were very large and came down to our knees—especially on Cheryl, as she was so much shorter than I was. We were laughing so hard, we barely made it outside. We ran out and did a little twirl, laughing until our sides hurt! Our moms clapped and laughed with us until we quickly ran back inside. We put our own bathing suits back on and packed the other suits back into the box. In our minds, our fashion show was a huge success!

We had a blast that day trying on all the other suits. Nothing fit, but it was fun seeing all the different shapes, colors, and styles.

I've always loved trying on clothes, including bathing suits.

I remember one summer when my mom taught me how to sew. She sewed a lot; she made clothes for herself, but also for my brothers, my sister, and me. I remember making a tank top and a bathing suit out of some material she had left over. We got some sewing patterns at the local Ben Franklin store in Hastings, and when we came back to the cottage, my mom taught me how to lay out the pattern, cut it out, pin it to the fabric, and cut out the pieces. Then she showed me how to piece the fabric and elastic together with pins before running it through the sewing machine. After an hour or so, I had a new light-orange bikini. I was so proud! I headed straight up to the swimming hole to try it out.

I remember getting into the water and suddenly noticing a problem. The fabric of my newly made bikini "grew" when it got wet! It was some kind of stretchy terry cloth fabric that my mom and I thought would be great for a bathing suit. Needless to say it was not! I remember having a slight panic attack as it grew and began falling off my body I held it in place, got out of the water, quickly wrapped myself in my towel, and ran back to my cottage to show my mom. I opened the door and called for her. I unwrapped my towel and said, "Look!" and there was my bathing suit, hanging off my body, at least three times the size it was when I made it. She looked at me and we both just stood there, then burst into laughter!

When I think of the things, we wear on our bodies—clothes, bathing suits, even shoes—I think of different characteristics that we have. The Bible tells us to "clothe ourselves" with different characteristics or virtues. We wear characteristics like we wear clothes. There's a passage from Colossians 3 that tells us to "put on the new self" (v. 10), which gives me the image of outgrowing clothes.

I remember getting ready to go back to school; I put on a pair of pants only to find they were too short or didn't close around the waist. They were too small because I had grown. While I sometimes got new clothes for school, there were also times when I got hand-me-downs from my sister and jeans from my brothers and cousins. These hand-me-downs were clothes that didn't fit them anymore because they had grown. So, when the Bible tells us to put on the "new self," it's referring to things we learn through growing in Christ. These things are the characteristics that we wear like clothes. Look at verses 12–14 from Colossians 3:

"Therefore, as God's chosen people, holy and dearly loved, clothe yourselves with compassion, kindness, humility, gentleness and patience. Bear with each other and forgive one another if any of you has a grievance against someone. Forgive as the Lord forgave you. And over all these virtues put on love, which binds them all together in perfect unity."

Notice how it says to "clothe yourselves"? The Bible isn't telling us to put on a different bathing suit; rather, it is telling us to put on compassion, kindness, humility, gentleness, and patience. These characteristics show we love the Lord. It's like wearing a team uniform. The shirt will say the name of the school or team to which you belong. Anyone who looks at it will know where you go to school or what team you play for. The same should happen when we display these characteristics in our lives.

When people look at us, can they tell we are Christians? Are we wearing characteristics that reflect God and who He is? Are our actions pointing to Him? Do we give God glory in our lives by reflecting who He is?

Sometimes Christians display characteristics that don't fit. Like those bathing suits that Cheryl and I wore that day, sometimes we as Christians demonstrate characteristics that hang off us. Maybe it's as simple as swearing or using God's name as a regular word or as a swear word. Maybe we cheat, lie, talk about others behind their backs, post, or look at inappropriate things online. When we as Christians do things that don't reflect well on God, it's like wearing clothes that don't fit. Others notice it. It's as obvious as that light-orange bikini that grew three sizes the minute it got wet.

Let's look closely at what characteristics we are wearing. Are we wearing "clothes" that fit, or clothes that clearly don't fit? Are our lives filled with kindness, compassion, humility, gentleness, and patience? Or are they filled with complaining, cutting words, insensitive comments, mean posts, or swearing?

Notice the last section of this passage: "over all these virtues put on love."

Today, let's put on all these characteristics like we would put on an outfit, and then clothe ourselves in love as if we're wearing a big overcoat. Let's make sure these clothes fit well, so others can see who we are by what we are wearing.

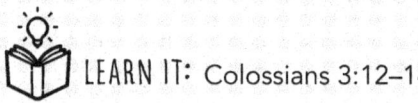

LEARN IT: Colossians 3:12–14

DO IT:

- Think about the characteristics in this passage: kindness, compassion, humility, gentleness, patience, love. Give yourself a rating between 1 (low) to 5 (high) as to how well you "wear" these characteristics.

_____ Kindness

_____ Compassion

_____ Humility

_____ Gentleness

_____ Patience

_____ Love

- When you get dressed today, imagine each item of clothing as one of these characteristics. For example, instead of something that says "Nike," it says "compassion" or "kindness." Wear that "brand" proudly and in a way that shows everyone you come in contact with that you believe in and support that brand. Others will believe it when they see it . . . when they see you being kind or compassionate. How will you show these characteristics? What can you do that will help others see them in you?

10. JUST WHISTLE WHILE YOU WORK (OR PLAY OR SWIM!)

I REMEMBER WHEN . . .

I LEARNED TO WHISTLE.

I don't mean just whistling a little tune; I could already do that. I mean whistling by putting my fingers in my mouth; the loud, clear, piercing, ear-splitting-if-you-were-too-close, hear-it-from-far-away type of whistle. The whistling that is cool.

It all started one day at the swimming hole.

My older sister Debbie had a friend from across the lake named Cindi and they had taken a fishing boat over from her cottage. We were all hanging out together at the swimming hole. Deb, Cindi, Cheryl, and I were out on the floating dock soaking up the sun when for some reason, Cindi put her fingers in her mouth and whistled. It was loud, clear, and super cool. To say we were impressed is an understatement, so of course, we asked her to teach us, and she accepted the challenge. The four of us sat there on the square dock in our bathing suits, sun beating down on us as she began to explain.

She talked and demonstrated at the same time. She took her first two fingers from each hand and touched the middle two fingers together. She then put them into her mouth, all four fingers touching the tip of her tongue. Next, she pushed her tongue back into her mouth with her fingers and blew. She told us and showed us how to situate our fingers in just the right way so that blowing through them would create a whistle. We all tried, tried, and tried until we got lightheaded and felt like we were going to pass out.

We kept trying, all the while chatting, baking in the sun, getting hot, jumping in, cooling off, climbing back on the dock, and trying some more. Cindi was a patient teacher and showed us her technique over and over. She analyzed it herself and thought of what she was doing so she could better explain it to us. We asked her all kinds of questions: Exactly where do we place our fingers on our tongues? And how far back did we have to push our tongues into our mouths? And what angle should our fingers be at to make a sound?

Cindi put her fingers back into her mouth and whistled, then tried to explain it some more and we tried again. Every now and then, one of us made a little squeak of a whistle and we all got excited, prompting us to enhance our efforts. This continued for the whole afternoon. Though we tried hard to learn, eventually the sun got the better of us. We jumped back in the water and swam to shore. As we wrapped ourselves in our towels, I tried some more, and Cindi kept giving me tips, saying I had to have my fingers in just the right place, or move them just the right way to get the air to pass through to produce a whistle. Each time I did what she said and got a little squeak, it made me want to try harder! We eventually went our separate ways, Cheryl and I doing our own things, and Debbie and Cindi taking the boat back across the lake to Cindi's cottage. But I didn't give up.

I kept working on it, day after day. One day, my brother noticed me trying, and since he also knew how to whistle, showed me a different technique. He told me to try using my thumb and forefinger from one hand instead of using both hands. He showed me how to make a circle with my thumb and pointer, put those against my tongue, push my tongue in and blow. So I tried his technique and kept practicing and practicing. My brother kept giving me pointers and within a few weeks, I could whistle! By the end of the summer, I could whistle with the best of them.

My whistle was loud, clear, and echoed across the lake. I got so good at whistling that my brother and I had whistling contests. We showed off all the many different ways we could whistle; thumb and pointer or four fingers—two from each hand. We could whistle with just our pointers, or just our pinkies. I remember whistling with each finger on each hand: four fingers, two fingers, and even one finger! We could even whistle using just one thumb to push our tongues into the right position. We were (and are) whistling masters!

My whistling has been extremely handy and helpful over the years. I remember at suppertime my mom asked me to call my siblings when they were either out on the boats or up on the point. I went out to the end of the dock, put my fingers in my mouth, and let out a whistle that rang across the water. It had a unique pattern that signaled to my siblings that it was time for supper. One of the families up on the hill had a big bell they rang, but our family had my or my brother's whistle.

When I had kids of my own, I continued to use my whistle. My kids would be out playing, but if they heard my whistle, they'd turn and look at me to see what I needed from them. I used it while teaching as well. Now that I'm a principal, my students know that whenever they hear my whistle, it means I need their attention. I whistle to signal the end of recess, for students to be quiet, or for my family to come in for dinner. I also whistle to call my dogs.

Whenever I whistle, I want someone's attention.

Here's the connection: God also wants our attention. He doesn't whistle for us, but He does a lot of things to get our attention. He wants us to come to him, just as I do when I whistle for my family, or my dogs, or my students to come to me.

Second Timothy 1 talks about how God calls us to Himself, especially in verse 9:

"He has saved us and called us to a holy life—not because of anything we have done but because of his own purpose and grace."

God calls us to Him so that we experience His love—both for our personal benefit, and to share it with others. When I call my family, it's generally because I want to be with them, or because we're going somewhere, or because we need to do something different than what we've been doing. Just as I call others for a purpose, so also God calls us for a purpose. His purpose for us is to live a holy life and to glorify Him. It's pretty straightforward.

Many people struggle with trying to find their "calling" or purpose in life or to understand what God wants from them, when really, it's pretty basic. He wants us to come to Him, experience His love, and share it with others by living lives that demonstrate what we need to do: *Love God and Love Others.*

He is whistling to you and to me! It's loud and clear and we can hear it from miles away. He wants our attention. He is calling us for a purpose: to Love God and Love Others.

 LEARN IT: 2 Timothy 1:9

 DO IT:
- How is God trying to get your attention?
- What does He want from you and how can you do what He wants you to do? Remember, it's not hard: Love God, Love Others.
- How can you do both of those things—not just think about them, but really DO something that shows your love for God and others? Finish the sentence:
- Today I will love God and love others by:

_____

_____

_____

11. SWEATING, SWIMMING, SUNDAYS, AND SABBATH

I REMEMBER WHEN . . .

WE WEREN'T ALLOWED TO SWIM ON SUNDAYS.

Sundays were enjoyable in their own way, but they were also a strange mix of "dos" and "don'ts"—rules that we had to follow that didn't seem to make much sense.

Every Sunday my family and many of our neighbors went to Gun Lake Chapel for church. I enjoyed Gun Lake Chapel mostly because of all the singing. I love to sing, and we sang a lot at the Chapel. It was a summertime chapel didn't have its own pastor. My dad preached the first and last Sunday of each summer; on other Sundays we heard preachers from all over West Michigan and Illinois who agreed to come out and take a Sunday service.

After church, we gathered at one of the cottages for "coffee." Everyone brought their own lawn chairs and baked goods to share, while the "host" made coffee for everyone. People ate treats and drank coffee and sat around and chatted for about an hour or so, then all headed back to their own cottages for Sunday dinner.

Most families had a big dinner on Sundays. We usually ate between 1:00–2:00 and then cleaned up. After dinner however, we struggled to find things to do. We weren't allowed to go swimming or use the boats on Sunday, because it was, well . . . Sunday. So we had to come up with things to do other than swimming, even when we were hot and uncomfortable, which was most of the time.

I remember when the older kids started playing whiffle ball on Sunday afternoons. They made teams and played in the front yards, close to the water. Home plate was facing the lake, so when the older boys went up to bat, they hit the ball so hard it flew over everyone's heads, past the docks and out into the water. The kids on the other team ran out the docks shouting, "I got it!" and then "innocently" fell into the water trying to catch the ball. They swam around trying to "find" the ball and then eventually hopped out of the water. By then, the other team scored a home run.

When the teams switched, the same pattern occurred. The players hit the ball way out into the lake, and the other team members jumped in to go get the ball. Obviously, the game wasn't about the points; I don't know if anyone even kept score. They just wanted to find a way to be in the water to cool off!

When we were kids, we didn't understand the "rules of Sunday." We all understood that it was Sunday and that God asked His people to rest on one day of the week just as He did when He made the world (Genesis 2:2–3). But that's about as far as we got. Even today as adults when we look back on those rules, we have a hard time understanding the reasoning behind most of them.

I remember my mom telling me about Sundays when she was a kid. She said her mom prepared the Sunday meal on Saturday, so all she had to do was heat it up in the oven the next day. That way she wouldn't have to "work" on Sunday.

Things sure have changed! Now Sundays can be some of the busiest days of the week. Getting a family ready to go to church is one thing; that's busy in and of itself. Then throw in sports, tournaments, and dance recitals and on top of that homework. All this can make Sundays very busy. However, it is nice that Sundays are still a day off; a day that's different from the normal weekday routine.

Generally, for Christians, Sundays are intended to be a day of rest. It's obvious that God ordered a Sabbath into creation. All of creation needs a time of rest! We see this in the 24-hour day, which has time for being awake, and time for sleeping. We see this need for rest in flowers that close up at night and bloom during the day. We see it in animals, as they too spend time sleeping. Think about bears and other animals who hibernate and rest for months! We see it in the seasons with trees that bud and bloom, and then enter a time of "rest," when the leaves fall and the trees go dormant. Creation was made to do its "work," but it was also made to rest.

The Bible tells us that God commanded his people to set aside times for the land to rest. Even today, farmers know that it's good to give a field a break from growing for a season, or to at least change what is grown in each field every few years. All of creation—from the birds and other animals, to humans, and even the land itself—needs time to rest and recover.

That's what was behind these Sunday "rules" that we grew up with. While they didn't always make sense, I for one knew that Sunday was set apart from the rest of the week. It was meant to be a special day. How that looked from family to family varied quite a bit, but Sunday was special.

Today, I wonder how many of us realize that this pattern exists? Are we intentional about working within the order God created when He built the need for rest right into how the world functions? Many of our lives are pushed and driven, and even middle school kids don't have time to rest. Between school, sports, dance, work, and homework, kids' lives can be extremely full. Add social media into the mix, and it seems kids never get to take a break.

So, what can you do this week to understand the need for rest? Looking back, I laugh about our Sunday rules growing up, but they did drill into us the understanding that Sunday was different—a day set aside to do something else, to focus on worship and family. Now that I'm older, I know it's not necessarily the day that is special as much as it is following God's order in finding rest.

Matthew 11:28 says:

"Come to me, all you who are weary and burdened, and I will give you rest."

Where do you need rest in your life? Do you need to rest from sports, dance, or social media? Take some time to spend time with God instead. He will give you rest for your soul and fill you up with His presence and peace.

 LEARN IT: Matthew 11:28

 DO IT:
- What do you need a break from? Is it social media, sports, or even homework?
- What can you do today or this week to let God refresh you so that you can go back to the wonderful opportunities before you renewed and refreshed and ready to roll?

_____

_____

_____

_____

_____

_____

_____

_____

_____

_____

12. SING AND SURRENDER

I REMEMBER WHEN . . .

WE SANG THE SONG, "I SURRENDER ALL."

On Sundays at Gun Lake Chapel we did a lot of singing. There were also soloists or groups that came to sing as well and provided "special music" for the service. I don't remember who they all were, but there was a great variety throughout the years, from large choral groups, to duets, to families who sang together.

Because the families around our cottage all went to Gun Lake Chapel, the singers as well as the preachers, were often a topic of conversation at "coffee" after church. Cheryl and I talked about the singers more than the preachers. I remember one time in particular the vocalist from that Sunday sang the song, "I Surrender All." This woman had quite the vibrato in her voice, so when Cheryl and I were back at the cottage, Cheryl sang the song and belted it out, sounding surprisingly similar to the soloist we had just heard at the Chapel. We laughed, giggled, and then, of course, thought we should probably give a concert.

So, just like our fashion show (only this time with more of our obliging neighbors in the audience), we held a concert. Two young performers singing acapella and by memory, "I Surrender All." We may have sung some other songs; I remember that one the most. There was one section where Cheryl held out the note and let her young voice, full of fabricated vibrato, ring out. It was a section that was repeated during each chorus, and she held it out every time we got to that part.

Our neighbors clapped for us and were gracious as we sang for them. They also commented profusely on how well we did and hid their snickers behind their smiles. Some could hide their laughter better than others could, but we were ok with that because we thought it was funny too!

As we sang the song over and over again, the words hit home a bit. I wasn't a fan of the tune, but it was perfect for holding out that one note toward the end. The words, however, made me think a bit more.

All to Jesus, I surrender
all to Him I freely give.
I will ever love and trust Him
in His presence daily live.

The first line was something I wondered about, as well as the chorus:

I surrender all
I surrender all
All to thee my blessed Savior
I surrender all.

That third line of the chorus was what Cheryl and I held out . . . "Bleeeeeeeessed Savior . . ." and with each chorus, the note got held longer and longer. I watched her closely to know when it was time to finish the word and move on to the rest of the song. She sang with her heart, and I followed along.

But I do remember thinking about the words and asking myself, in my everyday life, did I really surrender everything to Jesus? And what did that really mean? I *did* love and trust Him and live daily for Him. But what did "surrendering all" to Him mean?

All to Jesus I surrender
Humbly at His feet I bow
Worldly pleasures all forsaken
Take me Jesus take me now.

And these words too . . . Did I really forsake worldly pleasures? I liked our boats and my bathing suits. I loved the cottage and being at the lake . . . Did I need to "surrender" those things?

All to Jesus I surrender
Make me Savior wholly Thine
Let me feel the Holy Spirit
Truly know that Thou art mine.

I surrender all
I surrender all
All to thee my blessed Savior
I surrender all.

Growing up, I struggled with the things I enjoyed, trying to reconcile them with songs like these and my dad's mission work in India. I knew there was a disparity in the world around me; I saw the disparity between my own life and the pictures my dad showed us from India. I had so much compared to the people in India. I had clothes, a warm house, boats, cars . . . so much! And they had only the shirts or dresses on their backs. Whole families lived in small huts sharing one tiny space.

When I was 17, I traveled to India with my dad and saw that disparity firsthand. During the trip, we went to a conference in the mountain area in Punjab where the dominant religion is Islam. However, this conference was for Christians. One evening, people were sharing their stories, but I wasn't really listening. They were speaking with a strong accent and it was difficult for me to understand everything they were saying. Many weren't speaking English, and I didn't always follow along well with the translators. But then someone began to sing. The tune caught my attention and I listened closely:

All to Jesus I surrender
all to Him I freely give.
I will ever love and trust Him
in His presence daily live.

This man didn't belt out the words or the tune. He didn't focus on vibrato. He sang softly and gently, singing the words from his heart and with full understanding of what they meant to him.

I surrender all
I surrender all
All to thee my blessed Savior
I surrender all.

At that time in India, being a Christian meant that you may indeed have to surrender everything—your jobs, your home, your family and friends—for Jesus. Indian Christians were not always free to express their faith. Becoming a Christian meant they could be ridiculed, kicked out of their families, and possibly even killed. It was a very sobering thought for a 17-year-old American girl, hearing this song again in a whole new way.

I certainly didn't face any of those trials; singing "I Surrender All" didn't hold the same meaning to me as it did to this man. Even now, as an adult, my life is still so different from the Christians in India at that time. I still enjoy my family, the cottage, boats, my clothes and many other comforts. I know these are blessings that are here today and could be gone tomorrow. I just don't think about that very often. I begin to take things for granted, and sometimes I forget to be grateful for every little thing in life.

So, today, as I remember this song, I want to also remember Colossians 3:17 because it helps me to put things into perspective:

"And whatever you do, whether in word or deed, do it all in the name of the Lord Jesus, giving thanks to God the Father through him."

The Bible encourages us to live every moment for Christ, and maybe that's what the song refers to as well. Maybe this is the way I need to think about this song . . . maybe it's surrendering myself in everything I do, remembering that no matter what I do, I need to do it in the name of the Lord—and to give thanks.

 LEARN IT: Colossians 3:17

 DO IT:
- Think about EVERYTHING you do: eating, thinking, playing, schoolwork, social media . . . everything! What are some ways that you can honor God in EVERYTHING you do? Is it using positive language on the playing field rather than swearing? Or maybe it's being kind on social media, or being grateful for food, your home, and your clothes?
- Write down some specific things you can do to live out Colossians 3:17, and then do them.

_____

_____

_____

13. THE CREATURE FROM THE BLACK LAGOON

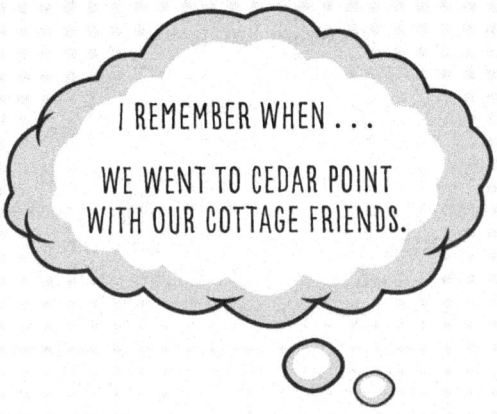

I REMEMBER WHEN . . .

WE WENT TO CEDAR POINT WITH OUR COTTAGE FRIENDS.

By the time we were in high school, there were more kids out at the cottage who were our age. Cheryl and I were now the "older kids" who had jobs during the day and came back to the cottage after work, just like our siblings had done when we were little. One day when Cheryl, I, and some of our other friends were swimming after work, we started talking about going to an amusement park in Sandusky, Ohio, named Cedar Point. We thought it would be a lot of fun to go together, so we compared our schedules and found a day that worked for all of us. We decided whose car we would use, and made a plan to leave at a certain time in the morning.

The park was about a four-hour car ride from the cottage, so we left at about 6:00 a.m. figuring we'd get there by the time it opened. The five of us all crammed into a small car that had no air conditioning and listened to the radio as we cruised down the highway.

When we got there, we rode all the rides, enjoying the roller coasters and water rides best. We ate snacks and walked around all day soaking in the sights and sounds of thousands of people having fun. It was a hot day, and we were sweaty and sticky, but we had a blast. When we finally piled back into the small car, we drove a while and then stopped at a random lake on the way home. We were so hot, and the water looked really good, so we jumped in and went swimming. It cooled us off and helped make the ride back to our cottages much more comfortable.

Hours later, it was dark and we were still driving when we came to a particular stretch of road that had some crazy curvy sharp turns. Cars have to slow down to about five miles per hour around those curves. We, being teenagers, were cruising down the road at a pretty quick clip, listening to music on the radio, wind blowing in through the windows not really thinking about the upcoming sharp turns. We were happy, tired, relaxed and still enjoying ourselves. As we entered the first sharp turn, my friend suddenly slammed on the brakes. The car came screeching to a halt. We sat there...completely still, lights shining straight ahead.

There, in the middle of the road, was the biggest, scariest, dark, creepy blob we had ever seen. It was huge! It was taller and wider than the car, and it loomed over us like the creature from the black lagoon. It felt like a real-life episode from *Scooby Doo*, only a lot scarier. As we stared at it, we realized it was just a hay mound, but it was so gigantic it was frightening. If we hadn't seen it in time, we would have crashed the car right into it. It was a close call and it set us all on edge.

Once we calmed down a bit from the shock, we inched the car forward and maneuvered around the mound of hay. However, the coast was not clear, because right before the next sharp curve, the car's headlights shone on three more monstrous, scary, blob hay mounds, all sitting there in the middle of the road just like the first one. It was as if the first black lagoon hay creature called his friends to come out of the woods and scare us even more than we already were! It felt like they had arms reaching out and over our car and big creepy faces with black oblong eyes and mouths wide open, screeching out their warning . . . "SLOooooW DOoooooWN!"

It was an eerie sight. Everything was pitch dark except for the headlights shining on the mounds of hay, so they glowed in the darkness. They were so out of place and so unexpected. Obviously, someone was sick of cars driving too fast through those curves and wanted to teach reckless drivers a lesson. Thankfully, we learned our lesson from the Scooby Doo hay-mound creatures. We were safe and we didn't crash the car.

Those hay mounds sure got our attention; I remember the sight as clearly as if I'd seen it yesterday. The thing is, I've driven on that road hundreds of times. I'd never seen anything like that before and have never seen anything like it since. It was the only time that ever happened, but I'll never forget it.

There are times—sometimes split seconds—that change the course of our lives. That night, we were simply riding along expecting to drive back to the cottage as we always did. But those hay mounds rose up out of nowhere and stopped us in our tracks.

Sometimes it's good to get stopped in our tracks. It's usually surprising, and it's not always pleasant, but it can set us on a course that can be helpful in the long run. That night, the hay mounds slowed us down. We drove much more carefully the rest of the way back to the cottage. We didn't speed, and we paid close attention to the road.

Things like that happen. The coronavirus pandemic has stopped us in our tracks as well. It's not pleasant; it's frustrating, and it seems to have come out of nowhere and stopped the whole country—even the whole world. But how are we responding? I know it made me slow down. It made me stay home more, relax more, spend more time with my family and even sleep a bit more. Those are all good things.

The pandemic has grabbed my attention. You see, God uses anything He wants to get our attention. He can use a beautiful sunset or a debilitating sickness to get us to focus our attention on Him and what He's trying to tell us. But no matter what bump or hay mound is in the road, He wants us to come to Him. We can come when we're overwhelmed with gratitude, or when we're overwhelmed with grief. He can handle it all. Thinking about all of the obstacles that can stop us in our tracks makes me think of the song "Give Me Jesus": "In the morning when I rise . . . and when I'm alone . . . and when I come to die . . . Give me Jesus." No matter what happens in life, He wants us to come to Him, in every moment.

I like how The Message Bible translates Matthew 6:34:

"Give your entire attention to what God is doing right now, and don't get worked up about what may or may not happen tomorrow. God will help you deal with whatever hard things come up when the time comes."

What is God using right now to get your attention? What kinds of things in your life are jumping out at you or stopping you in your tracks? That big old hay mound might look scary, but no matter what your circumstances are, turn your eyes toward Jesus and give your attention to what He's trying to communicate to you.

 LEARN IT: Matthew 6:34

 DO IT:
- Is there something in your life that seems scary or out of your control? Is God using it to get your attention? Write down the things that seem scary or out of control, then write down a few phrases and Bible verses to remind you that God is in control. Read through them every time you feel your fear or anxiety rising.

he allows it to happen
because he wants it to
happen.

14. KILLER PEACE

I REMEMBER WHEN . . .
IT STORMED AT THE COTTAGE.

It was always so cool watching the rain travel across the lake. The clouds got darker, and the wind picked up. I remember scrambling to grab the cushions off the deck and running out to cover the boats before the rain came. I remember stopping and watching as the rain came down on the other side of the lake. We watched the huge drops splashing onto the water. Our side was still clear and sunny, but the rain was coming. It was fascinating to watch it move like a wave toward us, getting closer by the minute. The rain beat down on the water, making it bounce as the drops fell.

Once it got to us, we ran inside and watched through the windows. Typically, the rain brought cooler air that cut the humidity and cooled off the lake. Sometimes, we stood out in the rain and let it soak us to the skin.

Rain was great for the lake. Day after day of heat made the lake feel like bath water. A good rain shower helped cool it down and make it more refreshing.

I remember when the rain turned into full-blown summer storms. We could tell how strong the storm was going to be by looking at the waves. These waves were very different from the ones created by the boats, and extremely different from waves on an ocean. Payne Lake waves were very small, but if they had "whitecaps" we knew we were in for a big storm. The whitecaps were waves that were actually big enough to crest and spill over (kind of like the waves at the ocean only about a thousand times smaller). The presence of whitecaps on our tiny lake meant it was super windy, or that there was a storm on the way.

I always enjoyed it when the rain and storms came streaming across the lake in the summer. They didn't last very long, and they were always cool to watch.

I remember one time I had a bunch of my friends from school out to the cottage. We were out in the boats, skiing, canoeing, hanging out in the water and having a great time when, out of the blue, a storm blew in. We quickly got the boats back to the dock and threw the covers on them. The rain had already started as we grabbed everything in sight, putting it all away because the wind was crazy. The rain pelted us as we cleaned up the yard. We ran inside, grabbed a bunch of towels to dry off, and watched through the windows as the rain came down in sheets. It got really dark as well, and we wondered if there was a tornado somewhere. When my mom was in college, a tornado came through her hometown and hit their farm. She told us some of her stories as we waited out the storm. She said a tornado sounded like a train engine, so we watched and listened. The power went out and it got eerily dark. It was scary, but it was also pretty exciting.

Because it was so dark, we lit candles and played a card game called "Killer." It had to be played in the dark, by candlelight, so even though it was the middle of the day, it was a perfect time to play this game.

Every player got one card, one of which was the Jack of Spades. Whoever landed the Jack of Spades was the killer. That person had to wink at someone without anyone else seeing it. Whoever was winked at had to silently count to three, and then drop his or her head, signaling he or she was "dead." If the killer winked at everyone before being found out, he or she won the game. If someone caught the killer winking at someone else, the killer lost the game. If a player accused another player of being the killer and that player was NOT the killer, both players had to be dead, giving the real killer an advantage.

We were ready to play. We all laid on our stomachs in a circle on the floor and placed a candle on the floor in the middle of the circle. The candle flame cast an eerie light on our faces as we looked at each other. We shuffled the cards and handed them out. Each person quickly looked at his or her card, then left it face down in front of them. Then the game began.

We slowly and silently looked at each other across the candlelight, eyes wide open and shifting left, right and looking straight ahead. Our heads turned to look at each other as we made eye contact and quickly looked away. The wind and rain howled outside, adding to the tension of the game. Sometimes someone made a spooky noise and we all snickered. We looked around, then someone's head dropped. Other heads turned, looking at the "victim." Lightning cracked outside and we all jumped. Another head dropped. The tension rose as we waited for the next victim. Inevitably, someone got silly, breaking a bit of the tension until others shushed him or her and got the game back on track.

We played many rounds of "killer" that day while it stormed outside. Sometimes the killer won, but usually the killer got caught winking at others.

Eventually the rain stopped, and the sky cleared. We all emerged from the cottage and started sloshing through the puddles in the lawn. The sun shone in the slightly eerie way that it does after summer storms. I remember just standing in the yard under the trees, looking around. It was peaceful and beautiful . . . the calm after the storm.

Storms like that remind me of the passage from John 14:27:

> "Peace I leave with you; my peace I give you. I do not give to you as the world gives. Do not let your hearts be troubled and do not be afraid."

We weren't afraid of the storms at the cottage, but we did experience the deep peace that came after them. During these times, I always felt like I needed to just soak in the silence, look around, and see the stillness in the wake of the storm. I remember looking at the lake, amazed that just a half an hour earlier there were whitecaps on the churning water, but now after the storm it was as smooth as glass.

There are times in our lives when the storms seem to rage. One thing after another just keeps piling on and it can be hard to find, sense, or experience any type of peace. But that's when Jesus calls us to come to Him. He is peace; He brings calm—not only after the storm, but also during it. He is also the One who calms the storm. When the storms of life seem to rage around you, go to Him and find the peace you're looking for.

 LEARN IT: John 14:27

DO IT:
- If there are things in your life that seem out of control, write them down then ask God to give you peace. As you talk with Him, write down some things that are peaceful and ask God to fill your mind with those things.

- We need to not try to "fix" every Situation.
- Peter & walking on Water.
- "he's already been to tomorrow"

15. HOLIDAYS AND CELEBRATIONS

I REMEMBER WHEN . . .

WE HAD POTLUCK DINNERS OUT
AT THE COTTAGE.

These happened a couple of times each summer. Some of the most memorable potlucks we had were on the Fourth of July.

On the Fourth of July, my mom's whole family came to the cottage. She had four sisters and one brother, and they all had a bunch of kids. Some of my cousins had kids of their own (my oldest cousin had kids my age!), so there were a LOT of people who came out to the cottage on the Fourth of July.

They came, bringing their own food, paper plates, utensils, and of course bathing suits. We borrowed picnic tables from all of our neighbors and strung them together across the lawn. Sometimes we had to set up two rows of picnic tables because there were so many of us.

I remember they started coming in the afternoon. Some of the guys wandered out to the dock, fishing poles in hand, while others grabbed a lawn chair and sat in the yard. The women brought the food inside the cottage, plugging in crock-pots and putting salads in the refrigerator and desserts into the freezer. There were coolers and picnic baskets everywhere. Things that could go right on the tables went outside on the deck.

Many of the family members quickly changed into their bathing suits—the younger cousins, older cousins, and second cousins—all getting ready to swim. The aunties and uncles, however, never went swimming. My mom and her siblings grew up on a farm in Hudsonville and they preferred to sit in chairs on the lawn, reminiscing and laughing together.

All the cousins, however, wandered up to the swimming hole and with a group that big, we always ended up playing keep away. We played for what seemed like hours, throwing the ball from the shore to the floating dock and everywhere in between.

Our neighbors often had friends and family over for the Fourth of July too, and the game would get even bigger as they joined us at the swimming hole. I remember some of the other cottage moms would also be in the water and when the ball dropped by them, we all shouted, "Throw it here! Throw it here!" The moms seemed oblivious but eventually one of them picked up the ball and tossed it into the mayhem. Kids were swimming, kicking, scrambling, pushing each other out of the way, and dragging others under the water to get to the ball. It was crazy!

Eventually we all got out of the water, wrapped up in towels, and made our way back to the cottage. Then it was time for supper.

We sat in our immediate family groups around the tables, with all the food each family brought on their own table. I remember eyeing my favorite dishes, hoping there would be enough left by the time I could get some. I also remember some Jell-O salads that people brought every year that were oddly refreshing while slightly nauseating all at the same time.

We all found our spots, and my dad opened with prayer. Then each table passed and ate their own food. It wasn't the type of potluck where all the food was on one table and everyone went through a line. However, that didn't stop anyone from getting up and going to a particular table to get something they really liked. We scoped out what our aunties and older cousins had brought beforehand, hoping there was enough to share. It was noisy, full of laughter and fun.

Looking back, I wonder if those Fourth of July celebrations with my cousins were anything like all those celebrations in the Bible. The Old Testament records many big celebrations—ancient potluck dinners that included whole people groups and the entire Israelite nation—not just a big family like mine! Exodus 23:14–16 talks about the Israelites having three celebrations a year: one in the spring, one in the summer, and one in autumn. The Bible also records big celebrations that happened when the army returned from their battles. Second Samuel 6:14–15 talks about King David returning with the Ark of the Covenant. It says that he danced "before the LORD with all his might." David was the nation's KING, and he celebrated by dancing in the streets! My family didn't celebrate like that, but we did laugh a lot.

Celebration is another wonderful thing that God has built right into humanity. We celebrate birthdays, holidays, marriages, and any other special occasion we can think of. It's good to be with others and enjoy each other's company. I've always looked at celebrations as a time to be grateful for the good things in life. Whether it's the Fourth of July or someone's birthday, celebrating a special occasion means that we are remembering it, and all the good things about it. God commanded His people to "remember" the many times He did something for them. He told them to celebrate and to build things like monuments that would help them remember the amazing things He had done.

The Fourth of July and Thanksgiving are national holidays that give us an idea of what the Israelites might have experienced in their national celebrations. Our celebrations are much different from theirs, but the joy and happiness and great family memories are probably very similar to those experienced by people in the Old Testament. People have been celebrating since the beginning of time; God encouraged, and even ordered, His people to celebrate His goodness together. Do you have any celebrations coming up soon? Any gatherings with friends and family? If so, enjoy!

LEARN IT: 2 Samuel 6:14–15

 DO IT:
- Think of something you can celebrate even if there's not a big holiday coming up. Maybe you can celebrate the fact that it's a certain day of the week, like Taco Tuesday. Plan a fun activity and then invite a few friends or even your parents or siblings to join in the celebration. Look up all the "National Day Calendars" and choose one to celebrate—national dog day, national donut day, or whatever. There's something for every day of the year, so dress up, make some great food, and enjoy the day! Write a description of your plans: What are you going to do? What do you need? Do you need anyone to help you carry out your plans? Jot down all your ideas and then make it happen!

_____

_____

_____

_____

_____

_____

_____

_____

_____

_____

16. FRIENDS

I REMEMBER WHEN . . .

IT WAS TIME TO
GO BACK TO SCHOOL.

It was a kind of strange feeling: the weather was still beautiful, and yet we were packing everything up and shutting things down at the cottage. It was still hot, and I always wanted to get in one last swim.

I remember lugging our things out to the car and seeing our neighbors doing the same. I remember conversations like, "when are you leaving?" and "when does your school start?" The thing was that all my neighbors lived in Michigan, and I lived in Illinois, so for us it was more of a big deal to pack up and head home. Eventually my family moved to Michigan, and then we went back and forth whenever we wanted. We lived so close that when I was in high school, I finished school for the day and drove straight to the cottage and went water-skiing.

But when I was younger, it was a bigger deal. I remember one time in particular, we all seemed to be packing up and leaving not only on the same day, but at around the same time. I remember we were yelling goodbye to each other across the landing, getting into our cars, waving and shouting well-wishes for the year and "see you later!" knowing we'd see each other again the following summer.

I remember going to the cottage one weekend in the fall and seeing my friend Cheryl. I never saw her other than in the summer. She sported a new haircut and was wearing jeans and a sweatshirt. I was dressed the same because the weather was cool. She was out riding her bike when our family pulled up to our cottage. I was so excited to see her, but at the same time, it was strange because I was used to seeing her in a bathing suit. It was kind of like seeing teachers in a grocery store—it takes a minute to recognize them because they're not in school. Cheryl in jeans and a sweatshirt at the cottage in the fall was a little out of context. But my mind quickly adjusted, and I was thrilled she was there. We went bike riding together and then went tramping through the woods. We obviously couldn't go swimming, but we still enjoyed being together and doing all kinds of other things. It was fun having her there.

Cheryl is the kind of friend that is a friend anywhere and at any time. Even now, almost 50 years later, we are still friends. I live a LOT farther away from Payne Lake than she does. We're both married, have kids, and have lived lives very distanced from each other. She bought her Grandma Babe's cottage and now lives there! However, every summer when I go to Michigan, she and I visit, laugh, and catch up on life. We still enjoy each other. No matter the circumstances, where we live, or how much time has passed, we're still friends.

It's not always like that. I've had friendships that have lasted for a certain period of time, and then we've gone our separate ways. Those friendships were great while they lasted, but there are many people whom I've never seen again after we've parted ways. That doesn't diminish the friendship, but rather helps me realize that life is precious. I want to enjoy each day that I'm given and to cherish the people God puts in my path. It also makes me value all my friendships even more.

There are, of course, friends who've hurt me as well. It happens to all of us and when it does, it's painful. This is different from when friends simply don't get along for a period of time. I remember times when Cheryl got angry or frustrated with me; it may not have been me as much as the situation, or something else going on, or that she was simply having a bad day. Either way, she'd be angry and I'd laugh, which made her more mad, but eventually, we always just worked things out.

But sometimes, anger doesn't subside and friendships get broken. There are all kinds of things that come between friends: we say things that are insensitive; we ignore each other; we make jokes at a friend's expense; we tell a secret that someone has asked us not to share; we say something about a friend that's partially true, but mostly not; we let misunderstandings fester. It takes wisdom and discernment to know how to work things out, and sometimes we just have to decide to move on. It can be difficult.

The thing about my friendship with Cheryl was that we always had to work things out. When we were young, there were no other kids our age at the cottage, so if we were mad at each other, either we'd end up spending the day alone, or we'd work it out so we could go out and do all the things we loved to do.

Friends are a gift. Just as Cheryl was a gift who enhanced my childhood, friends enhance our everyday lives. Today, people also have many "friends" through social media, which is a whole different type of friendship. Social media helps people stay connected when they don't live by each other. Through social media, I can see what my friends in Michigan are up to all year long rather than just seeing them in the summer.

God gave us friends because right in the beginning when He made the world, He said that it wasn't good for Adam to be alone (Genesis 2:18). In fact, the first friend He ever made was Eve. The Bible is filled with stories about friends, Jonathan and David being one of the most familiar. I imagine that having the king's son as a friend would have unique challenges of its own. You can read their story in 1 Samuel 20.

The point is it's good to have friends and to value them. Sometimes it's easy to take our friends for granted, and yet the memories we have with our friends and reliving those memories are some of the greatest stories in the world. Being a good friend takes work. It takes effort, forgiveness, and determination to work things out. It takes understanding of other people's opinions, views, wants, and desires. But the work is worth the effort! Friends are invaluable!

Think about how much your friends mean to you. Think about how boring life would be if you didn't have friends. Maybe you feel like you don't have friends. If that's the case, you can do something about it. You can be a friend to someone because I *guarantee* you there are others who feel like they don't have friends either. I know this because I see it every day.

Here's the problem: middle-school kids often think they have to have a certain kind of friend. They long to be a part of the "cool group" or be "popular"; they want to hang out with the "athletes" or some other subset of their class.

My advice? Don't fall into the trap of categorizing people as "popular" or "cool." If you want to be friends with people who currently aren't your friends just because they seem "cool," you're probably missing out on some amazing people right in front of you. And these are people who'd love to be friends with you. There are a lot of people who have a lot to offer. They might not have a lot of friends either, but I know they'd desperately love to have a friend too.

Open your eyes. Don't put others in a box. Reach out and be a friend to someone. Give others the chance to be a friend to you.

Friends are an amazing thing to have in our lives. And you know what? Not one of them is perfect. But then again, neither are you. Just so you know, the old cliché happens to be true: the best way to have a friend is to be a friend.

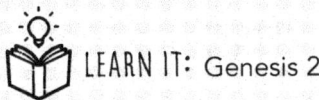

LEARN IT: Genesis 2:18

DO IT:

- Write down the names of three people in your life who seem like they could use a friend. Think of and write down ways to be a friend to one or more of those people.
- Choose a couple of things that you can do, and go be a friend to someone! Invite someone over after school, smile and say hello to someone, eat lunch with someone, ask someone to join in a game on the playground. The possibilities for making new friends are endless.

Pray for all Staff

17. LEAF BOOKS

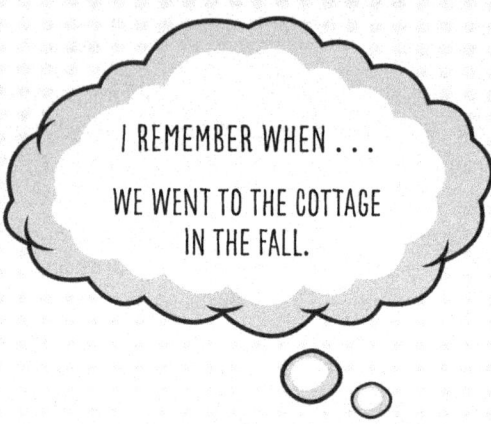

I REMEMBER WHEN . . .

WE WENT TO THE COTTAGE
IN THE FALL.

I loved going to the cottage in the fall. The trees blazed with color! I used to go for long walks in the woods to collect leaves. I tried to find the prettiest ones—fiery oranges, reds, and yellows. I wanted them to be whole leaves, with nothing broken or chipped away. I picked up one after another, choosing ones with the most vibrant colors and interesting shapes. I had a whole pile of them by the time I got back to the cottage.

I was so excited to show my mom all my beautiful leaves. Together we found big heavy books to put the leaves in, sliding them between the pages. Then, we set more books on top to add weight.

After a day or two, we checked on the leaves. If they weren't completely flat, we left them for a few more days. We waited until they were as thin as paper, then they were ready for the next step.

My mom got out waxed paper, an ironing board and iron. We took each leaf and laid it between two sheets of waxed paper, then covered it with scrap fabric and gently ran the iron over it, which sealed the leaf in the paper, protecting and preserving each one. I put the waxed paper pages back to back, added a construction paper front and back cover, and then bound all the pages together with yarn. Then, I looked at my "book" of all my colorful leaves, glad they weren't crumbling in my hands.

I was enthralled by the beauty of the leaves; I loved pressing them in the big heavy books and then sealing them in the waxed paper. I also remember, in the winter, taking a book out of the cupboard, rifling through the pages, and seeing a forgotten leaf drift slowly to the floor. I'd pick it up and look at it, so fragile and thinner than paper, the colors still blending into one another.

We all have ways that we preserve things or remember them so we can look back on them: scrapbooks, collections, journals, photo albums, social media posts, and the like. The Bible tells us that "remembering" is a good thing. Over and over in scripture, God's people were instructed to remember the things He had done for them, whether it was taking them out of Egypt or remembering His goodness and mercy from generation to generation.

My leaf collections were a preserved memory. Thinking about them now reminds me of the many good times I had when I was a child. They remind me of God's faithfulness, as each year I found beautiful new leaves to press and save. When I found old leaves pressed in books, they reminded me of how, as a child, I had God's Word pressed into my heart.

Psalm 119:11 talks about hiding God's word in our hearts: "I have hidden your word in my heart that I might not sin against you." I often hear students complain about memorizing Bible verses, but these memorized verses come back to us at unique times. There have been many times as an adult when I've been somewhere, or have been going through some particular trial, or even an amazing experience, when I have remembered a passage that is fitting to the occasion.

For example, I remember going on a gorgeous hike in Nova Scotia. During the hike, Psalm 100 started running through my brain on autopilot. It was so strong in my head that my brain started to put the words together with a tune, which eventually became a song. When we got back from our hike, I wrote it down and had a friend add some piano music to the tune. We then taught it to my students and they sang it in one of our school concerts.

I also remember another time when some scripture I had memorized came back to me. I was going through a really rough time; some of my good friends had said nasty things about me to a lot of people. I remember waking up in the middle of the night. I was so upset. I was crying and praying, and then Zephaniah 3:17 came to my mind:

"The Lord your God is with you,
    He is mighty to save.
He will take great delight in you,
He will quiet you with His love,
He will rejoice over you with singing."

This verse from my memory reminded me that God was there, quieting me with His love. It made me feel like I was wrapped in a blanket and held in loving arms. I was grateful that it was preserved in my brain.

I have so many memories of times when I didn't have a Bible with me, but I had God's word "hidden in my heart." It was there inside me, in my brain—in my memory, but also in my heart. It was there when I needed it, when I didn't realize I needed it, and when I actively tried to remember it.

I memorized a lot of Bible verses as a child, and so did my kids. Now those verses serve me well. Even as I write, I can remember whole passages, as well as parts of verses that are applicable to what I'm writing. That wouldn't be happening if my mind was void of scripture and if I hadn't put in the work and spent the time to memorize those passages.

Think back to those leaves, pressed carefully between the pages of all those books. To me, those leaves are like the scripture verses pressed into my mind. They are beautiful, rich, and well preserved. And while a leaf might not be of much value, scripture is worth more than the most precious metal or stone. In fact, the Bible talks about that too! Psalm 19:7–11 says, "The decrees of the LORD are firm, and all of them are righteous. They are more precious than gold, than much pure gold." You can carry those literal riches with you every single day.

So, when you get a chance to memorize some scripture, do it with your whole heart and mind. It will be there for you someday when you least expect it, or when you most need it. If you've never memorized any Bible verses, start today. Here are a few good ones to start with:

- Psalm 100
- Psalm 8
- Romans 8:28
- Romans 8:31
- Romans 8:37–39

Start preserving God's word in your heart today! It's much more valuable than a pretty leaf preserved in a book.

 LEARN IT: Psalm 119:11

 DO IT:
- Choose three passages to memorize and write them out here to start learning them. Next, write them on small pieces of paper and put them in your pocket. Take one out and read it any time you put your hand in your pocket. See if you can say the verse without looking at it. Also, share what you're learning with someone else.

_____

_____

_____

_____

_____

_____

_____

_____

18. ICE FISHING, ICE SKATING AND FINDING YOUR SWEET SPOT

I REMEMBER WHEN . . .

WE WENT TO THE COTTAGE IN THE WINTER.

A couple of times when I was growing up, our family spent our whole Christmas break at the cottage. It was great. The snow made the cottage look like a completely different world from the one I knew in the summer. Our tiny little place had transformed into a magical, warm haven in the midst of the Michigan winter's snow and ice.

I remember the long three-hour drive from Illinois to Michigan. We opened the door to the cottage and it always felt colder inside than it was outside! My dad turned up the heat and then built a fire in the fireplace. The heat took a little while to get going, but the fire quickly crackled and soon roared, heating the tiny cottage up nicely. I remember the small bedrooms were still cold because we kept the doors shut to keep the heat in the main living area. The whole place was so small that it didn't take long for it to be toasty and warm.

It was so cozy! The beautiful, clean, clear snow sparkled outside and the warm fire crackled inside. It felt like a winter paradise. The lake was frozen and we brought our ice skates, and I couldn't wait to go skating! My brothers liked playing hockey and my dad liked to ice fish. He even took me with him once . . . well, he tried . . .

I remember he and my mom bundled me all up so I'd stay warm. I felt like the little kid in the movie "A Christmas Story" who was so bundled up that when he fell down, he couldn't get up again. I had on my boots, snow pants over long johns, jeans, heavy socks, undershirt, tee shirt, sweatshirt, coat, scarf, mittens, and hat—and it seemed like there were at least two more layers I wasn't even aware of.

Anyway, I remember being all bundled up and helping my dad haul all his gear out onto the lake. I remember walking all the way out to the middle of the lake, and then casually mentioning that I had to go to the bathroom. I must have been pretty young, because he didn't tell me to just walk back to the cottage by myself. He sighed and took me by the hand, and we walked all the way back to the cottage where I got as unbundled as needed to be able to use the bathroom.

Using the bathroom at the cottage in the winter was a whole other experience—not only because of being all bundled up, but also because we didn't turn on the water in the winter. We brought our own water and used melted snow for things like, well, using the bathroom. We had this portable potty. It was a box that we put into the bathroom. I remember it had a blue, green, and yellow plaid decoration on the outside. When we opened the box, there was a toilet seat and under the toilet seat was a bucket. My dad filled the bucket up with snow to catch our . . . well, you know. We kept the toilet seat cover down so it wouldn't stink too badly. My dad changed it out frequently as well. I never really thought about where he emptied it, but I'm pretty sure it was out in the woods behind the cottage somewhere.

Anyways, after I used our "winter" bathroom, I got all bundled up again and we walked back out to the middle of the lake. Once we were out there, we got everything set up. There was a lot of gear for ice fishing. My dad had a big bucket holding some of the gear, and he had a funky wooden box to sit on while he fished. First he hauled out his auger—a long tool with sharp, round cutting edges, like a massive drill. He showed me how to turn the auger to drill a hole into the ice. It was so cool seeing the auger turn round and round, making a perfect hole right through ten to twelve inches of thick ice. Then he showed me how to use a big ladle to get the crushed ice out of the hole. This wasn't too hard, so he let me do it while he drilled another hole a little ways away.

I was thrilled to be scooping the crushed ice out of the hole. I put the ladle into the water and scooped out my first scoop. There was a lot of crushed ice, and it took a lot of scooping to get all the ice out of the hole. I remember seeing the other holes in the ice, watching him scoop out the ice and watching the water fill the hole again. Anyways, this time it was my job to scoop, so I kept going. I put the ladle in the hole and scooped out another pile of ice. I put the ladle back into the hole, but...it somehow slipped out of my mitten. I remember watching it sink down into the hole. I couldn't really grab for it because my hands were stuffed into my mittens and the water was icy. I just watched it disappear into the inky black water. Once it was completely gone, I called over to my dad and said, "Hey Dad! The ladle fell down the hole."

I remember him looking up at me, then dropping his head and letting out another great sigh. Then he walked over to me, took me by the hand and once again led me back to the cottage. I'm not sure what he said to my mom, but that was the end of ice fishing for me that day.

I remember watching him head back out to his ice fishing gear a third time. However, I wasn't going to let these minor mishaps stop me. I strapped on my ice skates—likely with the help of my mom because I probably couldn't bend down enough to do it myself—and I skated back out to where my dad was fishing. I remember skating in circles all around him. I worked on my figure 8's and twirls and all kinds of other tricks as he sat quietly with his little fishing pole (it was always funny to me how small those little ice fishing poles were). But, we finally found our happy place: Dad fishing, and me skating.

Looking back, it's funny how many little mishaps happened. The thing is, that's all they were: little mishaps. So often, I see kids want to give up when they run into little mishaps or experience setbacks. It's easy to think these little mishaps are enough to kill the fun. I'm sure my dad had had enough of me interrupting his ice fishing. But I wanted to be outside and on the ice with my dad, so I kept going out there and finally found my sweet spot. It wasn't ice fishing; it was ice skating! And I could still be with my dad. I didn't let the little things that got in the way stop us from spending time together.

This kind of reminds me of the story of the farmer who threw out the seed in Matthew 13. He experienced all kinds of mishaps and setbacks: the seed fell on the road and got eaten; it fell in the rocks and didn't get any nutrients; it fell into the weeds and got choked. Talk about setbacks! Verse 8 says, "Still other seed fell on good soil, where it produced a crop—a hundred, sixty or thirty times what was sown." It may have taken a little work, but the farmer eventually found the sweet spot for the seed to grow. I realize this passage is talking about people and God's word, but the seed analogy works too!

The thing is, perseverance is working at something until you find your sweet spot. Giving up too soon by letting mishaps and setbacks stop you from what you want to do will keep you from the joy of accomplishment and growth.

Where do you need to persevere in your life? Are you giving up too soon? What would you really like to do or try that needs a little more attention and perseverance?

Stay strong and persevere. The rewards are great.

LEARN IT: Matthew 13:8

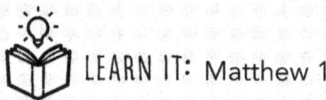 **DO IT:**

- Write down three things that you've "failed" at recently. Think about how you can try each one of these things again. How can you do something a little differently to get a different result?
- What is one area that you know is your "sweet spot"? Why do you enjoy this area and how did you discover it?
- How can you take what you know about your "sweet spot" and apply that to some other challenging areas in your life?

_____

_____

_____

_____

_____

_____

_____

_____

_____

_____

_____

_____

19. POPCORN GARLAND AND CHARLIE BROWN

I REMEMBER WHEN . . .

WE HAD CHRISTMAS
AT THE COTTAGE.

When we had Christmas at the cottage, we celebrated an early Christmas in Illinois and opened our presents there. Even though we didn't open presents, it was still Christmas, and I wanted the cottage to look like Christmas. I LOVED Christmas! So one year I asked my mom if we could get a tree and make decorations.

Because the cottage was, at that time, kind of out in the middle of nowhere, we didn't just go buy a tree or any decorations. We put on our winter clothes, climbed over the fence across the road and tramped into the woods behind the cottage. It didn't take long to find a perfect "Charlie Brown" tree. My dad cut down a tiny sapling with delicate needles. It was so small, he just picked it up and carried it back through the woods and lifted it over the fence. Then he found a bucket, filled it with some sand or dirt and stuck the tree in so it would stand up.

I loved that tree. It was small, wobbly, and just barely stood up in that bucket. We found some Christmas lights in one of the very top kitchen cupboards. We strung the lights on the tree, readjusting every time a branch started to droop under the weight of the lights. We cut some construction paper into strips and made a colorful paper garland to add to the tree.

I remember seeing TV shows and after-school movies showing people making long strings of popcorn garland. I always thought popcorn garland looked so cool on Christmas trees, so I asked my mom if we could make some. We popped the popcorn, and my mom got out a needle. I pulled out a LOOONGGG piece of string, figuring we wanted the popcorn to go around the tree several times.

I took the first piece of popcorn and stuck my needle into it, but the piece of popcorn fell apart in my hands. So I ate the little pieces and took another piece, and put the needle into a different section of the kernel, trying a different approach. This worked a little better and I successfully strung one piece of popcorn. The next one fell apart, so I ate that too, as did the third, fourth, tenth, thirteenth . . . and so on. After about a half an hour of trying to string popcorn, and only having four kernels successfully strung, I was getting frustrated. My mom saw me struggling to string the popcorn, so she offered to give it a try. It was slightly satisfying to see that she didn't have any more success with the popcorn than I did. So our tree didn't get any popcorn, but we did! We ate the rest and moved on to making different decorations.

We took out some old clothespins that we used in the summer to hang out our towels and bathing suits on the clothesline by the garage. We used the clothespins to make wise men, shepherds, and angels. My mom and sister and I cut out tiny clothes and glued them onto the clothes pins. We took a marker, drew little faces on the "heads," and added yarn for hair; we even made tiny crowns for the wise men. We used cotton balls for the sheep, and we used some of the construction paper to make wings for the angels. We added little arms holding little presents (for the wise men) and staffs (for the shepherds). We glued pieces of ribbon on the backs and when they were all dry, we hung them on our tiny tree.

I remember my mom told us to find some milkweed pods in the woods. We picked them and she cleaned them out. They were pointed at the top, then curved down on each side like a raindrop. The inside was curved as well, and she painted the inside gold. On the outside, she took some shiny silver rickrack ribbon and glued it around the outside of the opening. She added a ribbon to the top and used some other decorations she found in her sewing box. These milkweed pod ornaments were so pretty. They added a little class to our "Charlie Brown" Christmas tree. Overall, it was one of the most perfect Christmas trees that I remember from my childhood.

That Christmas at the cottage was right out of a storybook. It had none of the crazy materialism that fills our lives. It was homemade, quiet, and simple.

Sometimes we get caught up in all the shiny things of life and forget about the basic good things that don't cost any money—things that don't need batteries replaced, or the latest upgrade. There's nothing wrong with these shiny things unless they take our focus off of what is really important. If we live for the next latest and greatest toy— whether it's a phone, a gaming system, a boat, clothes, or whatever—we often can miss out on some of the most basic and most meaningful joys in life.

Sometimes it's good to strip away all the trappings and enjoy what's simple. Think about how Jesus came to earth: there wasn't a hospital for Him to be born in. There weren't doctors and nurses on hand in a fully cleaned and sanitized room. He wasn't wrapped in a Baby Gap blanket, and Mary and Joseph didn't need a fancy car seat to take him home. He was born in a stable; his arrival was simple and probably fairly quiet, other than a few animals sniffing and snorting in the background. And he slept in a homemade manger.

Luke 2 tells the story of where Jesus was born:

> "So Joseph also went up from the town of Nazareth in Galilee to Judea, to Bethlehem the town of David, because he belonged to the house and line of David. He went there to register with Mary, who was pledged to be married to him and was expecting a child. While they were there, the time came for the baby to be born, and she gave birth to her firstborn, a son. She wrapped him in cloth and placed him in a manger, because there was no guest room available for them" (vv. 4–7).

I know this is a well-known passage and we all love seeing the little kids act it out at Christmas. But when we really think about this, when we actually realize how stripped-down the surroundings were, it's pretty amazing. The Savior of the world didn't need any of the trappings of the world. Yes, the wise men brought some pretty amazing gifts to him later on, but when He was born, Jesus and his family were in a barn. Not even a cozy cottage—a barn. Talk about basic!

So, what do we learn from this? These stories are a good reminder to us to give ourselves a "greed check." It's fine to want things and to have nice things, but when they are all we think about and strive for . . . when they consume our minds, our time, and our money, we might have to take a step back and refocus on what really matters in life.

Remember the simplicity of the stable where Jesus was born. Remember the simplicity of that one quiet Christmas at the cottage. Understand that finding our contentment in God is something to strive for. God created us to need Him, and when we become too reliant on "things" to satisfy us, we start to feel empty rather than full. God is the one who fills us.

Have you ever watched, "A Charlie Brown Christmas"? In it, Charlie Brown struggles to find the real meaning of Christmas. He visits Lucy, the "doctor"; he directs the community play; he gets a Christmas tree, but the scrawny little tree is an embarrassment. Finally in frustration he cries out, "Isn't there anyone who can tell me what Christmas is really all about?" And that's when the wise Linus walks out on stage with his blanket, asks for the lights, and recites Luke 2.

As Charlie Brown listens, he remembers and realizes that Christmas isn't about glitter and bling. It's about the gift of Jesus—that one, simple, quiet gift of God's Son coming into the world. That one gift changes literally everything for those who believe in Him.

Christmas, and all of life, is really all about Jesus. No matter the season, the time, or the age, Jesus is the main thing. He came, He loves, He wants us to love Him and others.

So today, remember: Love God and love others. That's what it's all about.

 LEARN IT: Luke 2

 DO IT:

- Write down five material things that you want or have. Are they getting in the way of loving God and others even if they're not inherently bad?
- How can you strip away some of the materialism and get to the basics? Can you give some of your worn clothes to a shelter? Can you talk to a friend and encourage him or her rather than spending that time on social media?
- What are some other basic ways to love God and love others? Write out ten and then go do at least five of those ten.

_____

_____

_____

_____

_____

20. THE SNOW BUNNY AND THE SWIMMING HOLE

I REMEMBER WHEN . . .

WE WENT TO THE COTTAGE FOR SPRING BREAK.

That year, spring break included Easter, and every Easter we traveled to Michigan because my dad preached at different churches. This spring break we stayed at the cottage for the whole week!

During that week, right around Easter, there was a massive snowstorm. I remember it well, because my Easter dress was more "springy" and didn't really fit with the snow and cold! I had to wear a heavy coat over my dress, and I wasn't pleased. I wanted to be able to show off my new dress. However, wearing my new dress only lasted a couple of hours, while playing in the snow lasted all week.

I loved being at the cottage when it snowed. The snow made everything look magical. It was cozy inside and a blanket of white outside.

Most spring snowstorms drop some snow, but the snow doesn't last because the ground is no longer frozen. Not so the year we spent spring break at the cottage. The sky opened up and dumped more snow than we had had all winter! It was the perfect snowstorm, leaving us with perfect conditions: warm enough to play outside; cold enough to have a ton of snow, and the snow was wet enough to build our snow bunny! Because it was Easter, my siblings and I made a giant snow *bunny*, rather than a snowman.

It was the biggest bunny ever—at least it was for us. We made the snow bunny as if it were lying in the grass. He had a round tail and tall ears. My dad hoisted me up so I could sit on his back. He was big and sturdy, and he lasted the whole week without melting.

I remember the very next year, we went to the cottage again for Easter. My dad was preaching at some Michigan church as usual, so of course we stayed at the cottage. While we were there, we reminisced about our snow bunny from the previous year. It felt crazy that this spring there was no snow. It was too warm for snow; actually, it was hot—so hot in fact that we went swimming!

We put on our bathing suits and made our way up to the swimming hole. The dock wasn't out yet, so it was kind of weird seeing the swimming hole so bare. The milk jugs were there, floating at the surface and attached to the poles under the water. As we took our first steps into the lake, the water was so cold it stung our skin. My feet felt like they were in buckets of ice!

But we were determined to swim. Generally, in the summertime, we ran down the hill right into the water and kept running until it was deep enough to dive under. This time, however, we took our time, which was painful because the water was soooo cold. We didn't stay in the water too long, just long enough to get cooled off and brag about it for years to come! It was April after all; just a year before we had made that big snow bunny and now, one year later, we were swimming!

My family has often talked about those two years and how unusual they both were. Often, April in Michigan is just kind of cool and damp, but these were two years of extremes: first really cold, then really hot. The thing is, we enjoyed each one and adapted to the weather.

Weather is out of our control. There's literally nothing we can do about it. I remember just a couple of years ago going to Florida for spring break. I was planning on nice warm weather, so I'd packed shorts, bathing suits, and beachwear, and was ready to lay in the sun, get a tan, enjoy the water, and do fun "Florida" things. But this particular week was so cold, my daughter and I had to wear sweatshirts the whole time. It was overcast and a bit rainy. In fact, my friends who stayed in Massachusetts had warmer weather than we had in Florida! Our trip was not at all what we had hoped for. It was frustrating, but completely out of our control.

So what do we do with things that are out of our control, like the weather? Or a pandemic? Or sickness, divorce, or any crazy thing life throws our way?

To start with, we can think about our mindset and look at Philippians 4:11–13:

> "I have learned to be content whatever the circumstances. I know what it is to be in need, and I know what it is to have plenty. I have learned the secret of being content in any and every situation, whether well fed or hungry, whether living in plenty or in want. I can do all this through him who gives me strength."

This passage talks about being content no matter what situation we find ourselves in. Contentment and mindset go hand in hand. It's not always easy, but as we look at the passage, we see that Paul is a mindset master as he talks about contentment, or being at peace, no matter the circumstances. Good stuff, bad stuff, a lot of stuff, a little stuff—no matter what stuff, Paul says he's learned how to be content.

Contentment is a way to reframe our thinking. God can provide "peace" and help us manage our thoughts in the midst of whatever is happening around us. It doesn't mean that everything is ok, or even close to the way we would like things to be. It also doesn't mean we just roll over and take whatever is coming at us without doing something about it. It *does* mean God can help us shape our thoughts no matter what situation we find ourselves in. He may also provide some creative approaches to handling the situation.

For example, my family got creative building a snow bunny one Easter and swimming the next year. We embraced each crazy situation and enjoyed the time. I know this is a very simplistic example; however, I've seen people find contentment and peace in very challenging circumstances.

The main point? Contentment is found in God. It's not always easy, but He provides peace and can help us focus our minds to find contentment. If we find ourselves in a tough situation, it can help to realize that each one of us can be content in God while we either . . .

1. wait for our circumstances to change (because everything in life always does);

2. change our mindset on how we view our circumstances; or

3. get creative within our circumstances.

When we are constantly connected to God, relying on Him for everything, we can have peace and contentment even when we can't control the things around us. God can also help us with our mindset, just like Paul. It takes a lot of work, patience, and refocusing our thoughts and minds, but God is with us each step of the way. His promises are always at work; He desires that we focus our hearts and minds on Him so that we can find contentment that isn't dependent on our circumstances, but fully on Him.

LEARN IT: Philippians 4:10–13

DO IT:
- Look up some people who've had some rough spots in life and have overcome obstacles. Check out: Hellen Keller, Jim Carrey, Michael Jordan, Bethany Hamilton, Franklin Roosevelt, JK Rowling and Stephen Hawking, just to name a few. Read some of their stories. What are some lessons that you can learn from them? What is one of the things they all have in common? Did they let their circumstances keep them down, or did they rise up and make something great out of their seemingly crazy lives?
- They say "when life gives you lemons, make lemonade." So, go make some lemonade and while you're drinking it, think about one challenge you face and write down how you can turn that challenge into an opportunity to do something good.

_____

_____

_____

_____

_____

_____

_____

_____

21. CURLY CONE

I REMEMBER WHEN . . .

WE GOT ICE CREAM
AT THE CURLY CONE.

Once when my uncle, aunt, and cousins came to visit, they brought an ice cream maker! My siblings and I were instantly enthralled. It looked like a brown wooden bucket, and the grown-ups set it up in the kitchen. We used dry ice, which I had never heard of before, and carefully placed it around the little metal canister that was inside of the bucket. We put cream, milk and sugar into the canister, then made different batches and flavors using fruit jams, vanilla, peanut butter, and chocolate.

There were paddles in the canister attached to a large handle, and making the ice cream out of all the liquid ingredients meant turning the handle and churning the milk. Unlike the electric ice cream makers today that churn on their own, we had to do all the churning by hand. Churning the ice cream was hard work; one of us cranked the handle over and over until we were pooped. Then someone else took over. It was fun, took a LOOOONNNGGG time, and was worth every second of churning!

I remember tasting all the different kinds of ice cream. There were 11 of us, all crammed into the little cottage, making and eating ice cream!

Ice cream was always a staple at the cottage. We only made it that one time, but we generally had some in our freezer. However, the real treat was going to the local ice cream place, called the Curly Cone. The Curly Cone was a small ice cream shop right down the road. It was one of these great ice cream shops where you park your car, walk up to the window, place your order, pay, and get your ice cream.

As a kid, my favorite ice cream was a small twist—half vanilla, half chocolate. It was my "go to." My brothers got mediums because they were bigger and could eat more. My mom always got a scoop of butter pecan and my dad liked the lemon soft serve.

The Curly Cone was and is very generous with their sizes! It's funny when we see someone go to the Curly Cone for the first time and order a large cone. When the server gives them their cone, their eyes pop. They look at it astounded, and then they start licking the ice cream super fast so it doesn't fall over or melt in their hands. We of course know their cones are HUGE, so we plan and order accordingly.

I remember when we sat at the red picnic tables beside the Curly Cone. We licked our ice cream, chatted, and savored the time. Other times, we hopped back into the car and drove the short distance back to the cottage. If it wasn't too hot, we ate our ice cream a little more slowly and actually had some left by the time we got back to the cottage.

I remember the first time I ordered a "malt." It was like a shake, only it had malted flavoring in it. It tasted a bit like a "Whopper" candy and I loved it. I had a new favorite. It was thick and rich and creamy! When the "Blizzard" craze at Dairy Queen started, the Curly Cone added some new specials to their wonderful array of ice cream offerings. I'd get vanilla soft serve with peanut butter sauce and Oreos—all churned up into a Curly Cone version of a Blizzard.

The Curly Cone is still a thriving business. It has undergone a massive transformation since I was a kid, and it even has a website. The new owners moved about a tenth of a mile down the road to a new building. When I go to the Curly Cone now, all I have to do is turn my head ever so slightly to the left, and I can see the original Curly Cone, practically right next door. The new building has space where people can come inside and sit down, and they've expanded from being just an ice cream shop to a full restaurant that serves breakfast, lunch, and dinner.

We still go there for ice cream! My kids, too, have grown up going to the Curly Cone. It's one of those iconic places. My parents even went there when they were teenagers because my dad's family had a cottage on Gun Lake (right across the street from Payne Lake). If you look at the website and scroll down a bit, there's a picture of what it looked like when I was a kid. They even took the big sign from the original building and have it hanging in the new shop. When we have friends or family come to visit, we generally end the day with a trip to the Curly Cone. I even have a Curly Cone tee shirt!

I love the sweet things in life, like a cool ice cream cone on a hot summer day. The Bible talks about sweet things too, like how sweet it is to know God. Psalm 34:8 invites us to "Taste and see that the LORD is good;" Psalm 19:10 and Psalm 119:103 tell us that God's words are "sweeter than honey."

We don't often think of the Bible as being sweet. Ice cream yes, but Bible verses? Not so much. And yet there are so many sweet things that come into our lives when we know God and His word. Having a relationship with God is pleasurable, good, and sweet! Back when the Bible was written, the people of Middle Eastern culture were encouraged to use their senses to understand God and His word on a whole different level. This is why the Bible is full of metaphors. We know what it feels and tastes like to eat ice cream, and the Bible encourages us to "taste" God's word in a similar way—to know it's good and sweet.

Thinking about God's word this way is very different from seeing it as a set of rules and regulations. God's word gives us good things like peace, promises, encouragement, and hope for the future—all things good and sweet!

So today, go have an ice cream if you can. As you eat it, think about how sweet it is to know God. Think about the good things He has done for you. Taste the ice cream and focus on a specific blessing from God. Savor the sweetness and God's goodness at the same time.

Then share that sweetness with someone else. Find an encouraging Bible verse, write it out, give it to a friend or family member, and know that you are sharing the sweetness of God's love.

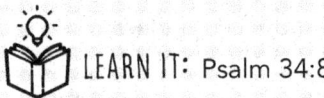

LEARN IT: Psalm 34:8

DO IT:

- How do you experience God's sweetness? How can you share God's sweetness with someone? Here are some ideas: Invite someone over who needs a friend. Have some cookies, ice cream, or play a game or just hang out. Your kindness and friendship will be the sweetness of God's love shared with someone else.
- Write out your plan: who will you invite? What will you do? Then, go make it happen.

_____

_____

_____

_____

_____

_____

_____

_____

_____

_____

_____

_____

_____

22. FEAR AND FREEDOM

I REMEMBER WHEN . . .

WE TOLD GHOST STORIES LATE
AT NIGHT AROUND THE CAMPFIRE.

I loved being outside at night. I loved sitting around the campfires roasting marshmallows and eating s'mores. I loved being with my family, friends, and neighbors. But I really didn't like ghost stories.

Ghost stories scared me—and not in the fun, adrenaline-rush type of way. For some reason, I thought about them for days and weeks. I thought about them when I was trying to sleep at night, and then woke up from nightmares. I just didn't like ghost stories. And many of them weren't even "ghost" stories as much as they were scary stories that had something of the supernatural in them. I don't remember many, if any, because I've worked so hard to get them out of my mind.

For some reason, my mind gripped onto those scary things. The scary feelings got deep into my mind, and the fear just sat there like a huge glob of clay. It wasn't like rock; it was more malleable than that. It was like a wet, sticky, heavy glob of clay. It just sat there, leaving me feeling weighed down and uncomfortable during the day and ridiculously scared at night. It was something I wasn't always conscious of when I was younger, but it was there—those scary feelings stayed with me.

I remember this happened when I watched scary movies too. I had a friend back in Illinois whose family loved watching scary movies and sometimes, I watched scary movies with them. Looking back, those movies were so lame and fake, but at the time, they gave me nightmares after I watched them. I'd wake up at night in a sweat, afraid to go back to sleep. When that happened, my mom always knew that I had watched another scary movie. They were so silly, but as a kid, the fear gripped me and held on tight.

I don't like to be afraid; as I've grown older, I've learned to protect my mind from unnecessary fear. I don't watch movies that are creepy, or scary in a bizarre way, or push way beyond a simple adrenaline rush. The same goes for books. I am careful about what goes into my mind. As an adult I've been afraid because of some silly things, but I've also had some very scary experiences. Still I know that if I allow myself to live in fear, then I'm stuck.

Fear can be debilitating. It can stop us from moving forward, and it can just sit in our minds like that lump of clay, always there, affecting everything we do.

Some kinds of fear are good—the kinds that affect our conscious and unconscious thoughts and keep us safe. For example, common sense tells us NOT to run across a busy street with cars speeding by. The fear of being hit by a car keeps us safe. The fear that comes from our intuition is also helpful. We may get a bad feeling about a situation that prompts us to leave and get to a safer place. God created this intuition in us to help keep us safe.

But fear can also get out of control and leave us paralyzed. There will always be circumstances and situations that are scary. If we let them, many of these circumstances could fill us with fear and control our lives. The "what if's" of life can cause fear: "What if I fail?" "What if I get cancer, or my mom or dad or siblings get cancer?" "What if I get in a car accident?" What if, what if, what if? This kind of fear can steal our joy every single day.

I remember being afraid not only of ghost stories and scary movies, but also of the "what if's" in my life. When my dad went to India every couple of months, I was plagued with "what if's": what if his plane went down, what if he got killed, what if he didn't come home . . . When he left, I cried all day because the fear of "what if" had me in its grip.

So, how do we manage our fears? How do we tame our fears to build wisdom and understanding instead of letting it lead to paralysis and worry?

I love this passage from 2 Timothy 1:7:

"For God has not given us a spirit of fear, but of power and of love and of a sound mind."

I love the words "a sound mind." That's where it all starts and ends—in the mind, or in our mindset as we've talked about before. When we ask God to help us control our thoughts, to take them captive each and every time they want to run rampant, we will find much more freedom and joy in our lives. 2 Corinthians 10:5 tells us that we can "take captive every thought to make it obedient to Christ," but doing so takes work. Choosing to defeat fear means relying on God and changing our thinking moment by moment. Freedom from fear is something worth pursuing, and it's a choice.

I choose to live in trust, hope and joy for each moment. When I let fear back into my life, it robs me of those things. I want to cherish every day. I want to be happy. I want to experience life, with wisdom and understanding—not putting my family or myself in danger, but also not being so safe that life goes by without me paying attention. I don't want the lump of clay sitting in my brain oozing into my thinking. I'd much rather take it out and make a mug or a vase out of it and fill it with tea or flowers. I'd rather make lemonade out of lemons!

How can you claim freedom in Christ and put away your fears? Even during times when fear abounds, what can you do to rein in your emotions and defeat fear? How can you "take your thoughts captive" and give your fears to God and then rest in Him?

God is the best place for your fear. He has you, and the whole world, in His hands. He doesn't promise that everything's going to be perfect, but He does promise to be with you every step of the way.

Do not fear. Walk with Him in power, in love, and with a sound mind.

LEARN IT: 2 Timothy 1:7

DO IT:

- Write down a few things that you are afraid of. Then, look up some scripture passages that help you focus your mind on God and on His promises to you. Next, write the scripture passage right over top of the words that express your fears. Uses this as a visual of how focusing your mind on scripture can cover your fears.
- To take this idea a little further, take some small note cards. Write these passages out on the notecards and put them on your mirror, computer, or any other place you look at frequently. When you see the passage, say it to yourself and refocus your mind on God's promises.

_____

_____

_____

_____

_____

_____

_____

_____

_____

_____

23. THINGS LEARNED FROM THE SWAMP

I REMEMBER WHEN . . .

WE WERE AFRAID OF THE SWAMP.

Our cottage was in the middle of six cottages in our "landing." Past our cottage, if we went up to the "point," there were six more cottages before the swimming hole. A paved road connected the six cottages on our landing. After that, the road changed to dirt as it ran around the point all the way out to the main road. Between our six cottages on the landing and the six cottages on the point, the road went right through a swamp. The swamp seemed to swallow the road with trees and reeds and cattails growing in the wet soupy soil on each side of the road. It was full of bullfrogs, poison ivy, turtles, and all things "swamp." It even smelled swampy with heavy air, algae-filled water, and leaves that gave off a thick green smell. All of us who lived in those twelve cottages even had a "swamp picnic" once a year!

During the day, we didn't think much of the swamp. Once Cheryl's family moved up to the point, she and I walked back and forth down the road that went through the swamp many times a day. Our feet got so used to the dirt road that we could walk barefoot on the gravel and not feel a thing. I remember walking through the swamp and seeing a snake slither across the road from one side of the swamp to the other. Snakes always freaked me and Cheryl out! We always screamed and jumped out of the way then stopped and waited for them to cross the road before we continued to walk. They were harmless, but the swamp was a home for all things creepy and crawly—or so we let our imaginations believe.

At night, the swamp seemed to grow bigger and scarier. It was pitch dark and our imaginations ran wild. Harmless turtles, frogs, and snakes became "creatures of the black lagoon" at night. There was only one streetlight of sorts, and it was really just a floodlight on the top of a wooden telephone pole by the sixth cottage on the landing. Once we passed that light, it was completely dark until we got up to the point. The swamp was pitch black.

Cheryl and I frequently went back and forth between our cottages. We were always a little scared walking down the road through the swamp at night—not because anything ever happened, but because it was just so dark and all those snakes we saw during the day were sure to quadruple in size during the night. Still, we had to walk through the swamp from my cottage to hers. When it was dark, we walked to the end of the pavement on the landing. We looked at each other, looked at the road going through the swamp, looked at each other again and yelled, "GO!" Then we ran full-speed through the swamp! Our feet sped over the rocks and our towels flew like capes behind us. Once we got through the swamp, we caught our breath and walked the rest of the way to her cottage.

There were also times when one of us had to go through the swamp alone. Many times, I was at Cheryl's cottage until it grew dark and I had to go home. Cheryl and I walked together to the edge of the swamp, bid each other farewell, and I ran as fast as I could through the swamp. Cheryl stood on her side of the swamp and called out to make sure I made it. I yelled back saying I was all set, and then we each headed off to our own cottages.

It's funny thinking about how scared we got as we ran down the road that cut through the swamp. I remember taking late-night walks with my dad and brothers. I held my dad's hand on one side, and my brother's on the other. When we reached the swamp, I was safely in between my dad and brothers. When I was with my dad and brothers late at night, we didn't run through the swamp. Instead, we looked up and saw all the stars, shining bright in the inky night sky. We could see thousands of them because there were no streetlights, house lights, or city lights. It was just the beautiful night sky.

But when it was just Cheryl and me, we didn't look at the stars. We heard all the sounds of the swamp and let our imaginations run wild.

The thing is, we never let the swamp stop us from going back and forth to each other's' cottages.

Here's some lessons I've learned from the swamp:

1. Make sure to go through the swamp because there are good things on the other side. It may be scary, but don't let that stop you.

2. Have a friend or two with you when you have to face the swamp.

3. When you're in the middle of the swamp, look up and see the beauty that surrounds you.

We all face scary things in life, and sometimes we just have to go through them. We can't escape them or ignore them. What's great is that God promises He is always with us! Look at Isaiah 43:2:

> "When you pass through the waters, I will be with you; and when you pass through the rivers, they will not sweep over you."

We can easily switch out "the waters" for "swamp" or any other potentially scary thing that we are currently facing.

In addition, having friends who are there for you is also a huge blessing and help. Look at this verse from Ecclesiastes 4:9–10:

> "Two are better than one, because they have a good return for their labor:
> > If either of them falls down,
> > one can help the other up."

I'm glad Cheryl was with me through the swamp, and I'm grateful for friends who continue to walk with me through tough times!

Finally, think about Psalm 8:

When I consider your heavens,
    the work of your fingers,
the moon and the stars,
    which you have set in place,
what is mankind that you are mindful of them,
    human beings that you care for them?

God is with us in and through whatever "waters" or "swamps" that may be in our lives. He is there every step of the way! Sometimes He is our friend who is there with us when we have to run through the swamp. At other times, He is our dad and brother, holding our hand and telling us to look up and see the beauty in the midst of it.

Don't let the swamp stop you, my friends! Walk through, hold on to God, and find the beauty!

LEARN IT: Isaiah 43:2

 DO IT:
- List the swamp or the deep waters you are facing. List the friends you have that have shown they are true friends.
- List some truths about God on which you can focus your mind when you face scary or challenging situations.
- Write down ways you have been a friend to others who are facing challenges in their lives. How can you be a friend to someone else and how can you ask a friend for help when you need it?

_____

_____

_____

_____

_____

_____

_____

_____

_____

_____

_____

_____

_____

24. HEAT, HOT, SWEAT

I REMEMBER WHEN . . .

IT WAS SO HOT AT THE COTTAGE
IT WAS HARD TO SLEEP.

We didn't have air conditioning at the cottage, and there were nights when there was no breeze. The heat from the day settled into the night and as much as I tried, I couldn't sleep. I remember we only had one fan, so my parents put it in the little area right outside our room, facing the fan into the bedroom. Even with the fan, some nights were still just too hot.

During the day, we went into the water to cool off. Even when the water got really warm, swimming in it was still a break from the heat. But at night, there was no break, just constant heat.

I remember how hot it was as I laid there, still as a board, sweating as if I'd just run three miles. It wasn't a dry heat either—it was muggy. When it's muggy, it feels hotter than it really is. I've heard of people in Arizona who live in 100 to 115 degree weather on a consistent basis, but the air is dry, and they typically have air conditioning. Michigan summers in the 1970's were hot and muggy, and I literally had to sweat it out.

During July and August when the heat was at its worst, the water in the lake felt like bathwater. We still swam in it because it was slightly cooler than the air, but it was hot everywhere we turned. I remember getting out of the water and feeling cool when the air hit us, but that feeling only lasted about 30 seconds. After the water on our skin and bathing suits evaporated, we started sweating again.

I don't like being that hot. I remember when I was older and had kids of my own, we visited my brother and his family in the Dominican Republic. It was beautiful, but again, the nights were HOT. I remember sleeping with my baby daughter next to me, a fan blowing directly on us, both sweating buckets. My little baby girl was covered with a layer of baby mist (also known as sweat); her fine hair stuck to her face, wet with perspiration. I lay there in the dark, the fan blowing air directly on me and sweat still dripped off my skin. Those nights I just laid there, hoping for sleep that wouldn't come because it was too hot.

There are people who are happier the hotter it gets—I am not one of those people. I like it warm, but once things hit around 90 or above, I've had enough. I'm kind of like Goldilocks: I like outside and inside temperatures that are "just right."

We all like to be comfortable; like Goldilocks, we all want things to be "just right." But God is not looking for Goldilocks. He's looking for people who are passionate about things. He doesn't want us to get complacent. He wants us to be either hot or cold, like in Revelation 3:15–20: "I know your deeds, that you are neither cold nor hot. I wish you were either one or the other! So, because you are lukewarm—neither hot nor cold—I am about to spit you out of my mouth."

Remember that being "complacent" is very different from being "content." When we're complacent, we start taking things for granted, aren't grateful anymore, and don't find value in what we have. We just don't care. I've seen lots of students get complacent in life. When things get too hard, they shut down and claim they just don't care. They get bored, disengaged, and unmotivated. I've been there too. It is a frustrating place to be. When we don't care, it's hard to be motivated and hard to get things done.

But God doesn't want us to be complacent, especially not about Him. Look again at Revelation 3:15–20. He wants us to be on fire for Him, and not "lukewarm." In fact, He'd rather have us be either hot or cold!

So, how can we keep ourselves from becoming complacent or "lukewarm"? In a world where we have everything at our fingertips, how can we stay excited, full of wonder, and passionate about God, His people, and His world?

First, we can't take any of it for granted. We need to be grateful every day of our lives, many times a day! We need to tell others about how good God is. We need to share with others how amazing He is and how much He loves each one of us. We also need to be forgiving and loving toward others, and content in all situations rather than complacent.

Second, we need to take time to appreciate the details in our lives, understanding that God is in the details. Think about all the amazing small things in life that we can miss if we're not looking: the petals on a flower, butterfly wings, eyelashes, spider webs, and millions of other things. Sometimes we miss or ignore them, but God is in the details, right down to the hair on our heads! Luke 12:7 says, "the very hairs of your head are all numbered," so look for and be amazed by the details!

Finally, read Psalm 139, which focuses on how God created us, and how intimate and detailed that process is:

> For you created my inmost being;
>> you knit me together in my mother's womb.
> I praise you because I am fearfully and
>> wonderfully made;
>>> your works are wonderful,
>> I know that full well.
> My frame was not hidden from you
>> when I was made in the secret place,
>> when I was woven together in the depths of
>> the earth.
> Your eyes saw my unformed body;
>> all the days ordained for me were written in your book
>> before one of them came to be (vv. 13–16).

Because he knows us so well, God is always with us, and there is nowhere in all creation where we can try to go and get away from Him (see vv. 7–12). He is everywhere. When we take the time to really think about and meditate on these things, they should shake us out of our complacency.

These days when I remember those hot days and nights at the cottage, I know that there were a thousand (or more) things to be grateful for, to think about, and to share with others. I had a cottage. There was a beautiful little lake to swim in. We had boats. I had my family around me. I was happy. Even when I was laying there sweating, there was so much to be grateful for.

So when life heats up and you want to shut down, remember to not get complacent. Instead, change your mindset. Be passionate about God and full of wonder at all the amazing details around you. Be ready to learn instead of giving up. Be ready to think and work hard instead of coasting. Be ready to be sweaty, and when you are, marvel at the heat and your body's natural cooling systems instead of just waiting for cooler weather. Be ready to stop and look at a spider web instead of just cleaning it away. Wonder, marvel, and be in awe about every part of life. That's how we keep ourselves from becoming complacent.

God is in the details.

 **LEARN IT:** Psalm 139

 DO IT:
- Write down ten things that amaze you. Choose two of those things and do some research to learn more about both of them. When you know some more about two of those things, share what you've learned with someone else.

_____

_____

25. BAREFOOTIN'

I REMEMBER WHEN . . .

OUR LAKE HOSTED
SKIING COMPETITIONS.

Skiing was a big thing on our lake and a favorite pastime. All of us kids skied, and many of us were really good at it.

At first the skiing competitions were for slalom skiing. I remember seeing a boat full of guys out on the water on a quiet weekday afternoon. The boat was moving slowly along the still stretch of water right across from our cottage. The guys in the boat would lean over the edge as they put in markers for the upcoming slalom competition. I remember seeing milk jugs floating in the water, marking each turn. They made sure they placed the buoys the right distance apart so each skier had enough time and space to crisscross between them. This whole process signaled the upcoming competition the following Saturday morning. When that next Saturday morning came, our lake was flooded with people, boats, and skiers!

I remember sitting out on our deck watching. Sometimes the participants started with some entertainment, pulling as many as twelve skiers behind one boat. I remember some teams made pyramids—the strong guys all skiing close together while the lighter girls climbed on to their shoulders. It was so cool to watch, and they were really good at it. I remember seeing ski pyramids on TV and thinking, "Hey—we do that on our lake!"

Next came the slalom races. I loved watching the skiers race through the buoys, crossing back and forth, cutting through the wake, water spraying a high rooster tail behind them as they turned to cross back to the next buoy. I'm not sure how they actually judged the competition, but it was always fun to watch.

Over the years, some of the skiers became so good at skiing, they looked for the next challenge: barefooting. Why use skis to water ski, right? It seemed so crazy at the time, but many of the guys on our lake learned to barefoot, and the ski competitions changed to barefooting competitions.

Barefooting competitions didn't need any buoys. The guys skied barefoot side-by-side behind a boat for as far as they could go. I remember watching them and hearing them talk with each other as they were basically standing on the water while being pulled by the boat. It was fun to watch because when they fell, they tumbled like clothing in a dryer—but it looked pretty painful!

To get started, they slalomed. When the boat gathered enough speed, they took their back foot out and put it into the water, heel down and toes curled up. They put their weight on this foot and then jumped out of the slalom ski, quickly putting their other foot into the water. Then they were "barefootin'!" They barefooted side by side until one of them fell. They had some sort of a bracket system, so the skier who fell moved down in the bracket while the skier who stayed standing moved up in the bracket. Individuals competed until the tournament had a winner.

Some guys became so good at barefootin' they could get up without skis. They laid on their backs in the water and held on to the ski ropes. They put their feet up, heels criss-crossed on the rope as the boat started to pull them. Soon they were zipping along on their backs, feet on the taut rope, hands holding tightly to the handle. Next, they put their feet down and popped up all in one fluid movement.

I always found barefooting amazing. Cheryl and I really wanted to be able to barefoot like all the older guys, so we tried it. I remember how the water felt when I put my first foot into the water. It tickled! The boat was going so fast that when I tried to put my foot on the water, balance, and kick the other ski off and rebalance, I fell . . . hard. Water went up my nose and my body tumbled like a rock going down a cliff. Water can be very unforgiving when you're skiing—falls like that hurt. I remember trying to barefoot a couple more times, but I didn't have a wetsuit like the guys in the competitions and I really didn't like falling that hard, so I stuck to using skis.

I love watching barefooting because it's a great example of people breaking through the conventional way of doing things. When people get really good at something, they eventually break through the boundaries and try something new. I had never even heard of barefooting until the guys on our lake started doing it. I remember going back to school and telling my friends about it and they were like, "How can you ski without skis?" I explained, "Well . . . that's why they call it "barefootin'." My friends had a hard time believing it, but eventually the sport became more popular and well known.

Barefooting and breaking boundaries reminds me of the artist Picasso. He was so good at painting realistically by the time he was a teenager that he had to try new things, break out of the mold, and get unconventional with his painting. He went through many methods of painting different styles until Cubism was born! (Look it up—it's pretty wild.)

It can be scary to try new things, especially things that have never been done before. But that's how inventions are created, and that's how new fads are generated. In order to break through convention, we have to be willing to take risks. Risks can be scary because they generally involve the chance of falling hard and failing altogether (or what people like to think of as failing).

I love what Thomas Edison said of his many attempts at different inventions: "I have not failed. I've just found 10,000 ways that won't work."

I don't know about you, but if I tried barefooting 10,000 times and had fallen every time, I would probably call that failing. But I LOVE that Thomas Edison didn't see life this way. He kept trying, taking risks, and thinking outside of the box. Because he did, he created many inventions that made life easier for all of us. He advanced technology that other people, in turn, advanced as well. And it worked! I'm grateful that he never gave up, and I'm grateful for other people who refuse to give up!

Such people remind me of the Israelite spies who went to look at the promised land. Numbers 13 talks of how these men came back with their report. Most of the spies were scared at the size of the people in the land, and they started spreading lies and rumors about their experiences. But Caleb, unlike the other spies, said, "We should go up and take possession of the land, for we can certainly do it" (v. 30).

Caleb's my kinda guy—he was ready to take the risk and had faith that God would deliver the land into their hands. He saw what was before them and was ready to take the risk and persevere. I love the part of the verse that says, "we can certainly do it." He had confidence! Maybe if he had lived in our time, Caleb would have learned to barefoot.

Today I challenge you to take a risk. Think outside of the box and try something new. You don't need to try barefootin', but don't be afraid to try something once, or ten times, or 10,000 times. And even if you find 10,000 ways that don't work, you might stumble on the answer on the 10,001st try! Decide to take a risk, and have fun!

 LEARN IT: Numbers 13:30

 DO IT:
- What is something you've always wanted to learn how to do? How can you start learning how to do it? What steps will you take? How will you push yourself to keep trying even when you don't get it the first few times? Write down the quote from Thomas Edison and read it when you feel like giving up.

26. EXERCISE AND ENDURANCE

I REMEMBER WHEN . . .

CHERYL AND I DECIDED TO SWIM ACROSS THE LAKE.

When we were kids, the fitness craze was just underway and people were running, swimming, and doing aerobics using videotapes that featured Jane Fonda and Richard Simmons (old technology and even older people!). Cheryl and I were already active, so one day we decided to swim across the lake. We had seen some other people doing it, and we were confident we could do it as well.

We were at the swimming hole sitting out on the floating dock. We were chatting and looking out at the lake and saw a floating dock directly across the lake. We always knew it was there, but this time it looked different: it was a target; a goal. Because it was the middle of the day the lake was quiet. The speedboats were all docked, and no one was out skiing.

So, we dove in and started swimming. We weren't really doing it for exercise; we just saw that other floating dock in the distance and decided to go for it. We swam and swam and swam. We were about halfway across the lake and looked back, then looked forward and swam some more.

We were both in pretty good shape because we skied so much, swam all day, and were basically outside and active all the time. But swimming a long distance instead of doing handstands and somersaults in the water was a whole different kind of exercise.

We switched up our stroke between freestyle, breaststroke, and backstroke. I remember when my arms needed a rest, I just swam backwards, kicking my legs. I remember kicking and kicking, enjoying the freedom of moving toward my goal while resting my arms. My legs and feet splashed and made little waves as I kicked. Eventually I heard something, so I stopped and looked around. Cheryl was calling to me, letting me know that I had veered off course. The problem with going backwards was that when I stopped and looked to find my target, it wasn't where I had expected it to be—I had been heading in a completely different direction! So I had to face forward again and get back into the more or less straight line that would bring me to my goal—the other dock.

Eventually we got there. We climbed up and sat on this dock looking across the lake back at the swimming hole. We talked about how our arms would be sore the following day (and they were)! We sat there chatting and looking at the lake from a whole different perspective.

We didn't know who the dock belonged to, but we weren't worried about that. We knew, however, that we couldn't stay there. We talked about getting out of the water and walking home, but we didn't have towels or cover-ups or shoes. So, after we rested a while, we dove back in and swam the distance back to the swimming hole.

We felt a sense of accomplishment and pride that we made it across the lake and back. The whole trip took a bit longer than either of us had expected, but we did it, and because we had done it once, we knew we could do it again. However, whenever we swam across the lake in the future, we always took a rowboat, canoe, or paddleboat. One of us swam to the other side while the other paddled the boat. Then we switched it up and came back.

It took a lot of endurance to swim across the lake and back that first time. The thing is, we couldn't really quit: once we were out in the middle of the lake, we had to keep going, either forward to this new target—the other floating dock—or back to the swimming hole. Either way, we had to continue. There was no other alternative. We couldn't just float in the middle of the lake for the rest of the day; we had to keep moving.

Similarly, there are times in life when we have to push forward and continue, when we can't just quit and stay where we are. Those times may not be pleasant, but they do build our endurance.

All athletes work to build endurance. While we all need to build up physical endurance, we also need to build mental endurance. Mental endurance takes over when our bodies want to give up. Mental endurance is listening to that voice—either from a coach or from inside of us—that encourages us to keep going and not give up when things get difficult.

Endurance gets us through the hard times and leads us to a reward. We need endurance in every area of life. Galatians 6:9 says, "Let us not become weary in doing good, for at the proper time we will reap a harvest if we do not give up." Sometimes it seems like we keep working and working for something but never see the end product. This is the process that produces endurance.

I love this version of Philippians 4:13:

"For I can do everything God asks me to with the help of Christ who gives me the strength and power."

Webster's Dictionary defines "endurance" this way: "The ability to withstand hardship or adversity *especially*: the ability to sustain a prolonged stressful effort or activity."

Swimming across the lake wasn't exactly a hardship and it wasn't stressful. It was, however, a sustained and prolonged activity and we couldn't just stop swimming. We needed the mental toughness to keep going when our arms and legs got tired. While many definitions of endurance link it to physical activity, endurance in mental challenges is just as important. When we fix and focus our minds, our mental endurance builds, giving us strong minds. The Bible talks about this type of endurance.

I remember studying for tests and writing long papers. Those types of activities take a lot of mental endurance. Focusing on tasks over a long period of time and pushing our brains to work hard builds endurance. While the brain is an organ, it also acts as a muscle. We can make it stronger, just like exercise strengthens our hearts and lungs. We can strengthen all the muscles in our bodies, but we often don't think about how we can build strength in our brains. But we can! We can strengthen them and build endurance by working hard, studying, and not giving up. We may need breaks, just like when Cheryl and I stopped swimming and gauged our progress or changed our stroke. Our brains and our bodies work in tandem as we strive to get stronger. Remember what Thomas Edison said about finding 10,000 ways that one of his inventions didn't work? Well, that was him building endurance! His hands didn't keep working without his brain pushing him to keep trying.

Building our endurance is not easy. In fact, it has to be hard in order for endurance to build! But I want to challenge you today to think about the two verses quoted above — Galatians 6:9 and Philippians 4:13. No matter what you're going through, don't give up! You've got this and God is with you every step of the way!

 LEARN IT: Galatians 6:9 and Philippians 4:13

 DO IT:
- What is something you have to work on that doesn't come easily for you? Is it a subject in school or something physical? Work to build your endurance. Go walk or run and go five to ten minutes longer than you normally would. Notice what it feels like to push yourself just a little to build up your endurance. Then, think about your mind and how it wants to give up at times. Push yourself to focus on something for five to ten minutes longer than you normally would. Write out your thoughts and ideas as you build up that endurance!

27. DRAMA, DRAMA, DRAMA

I REMEMBER WHEN . . .

CHERYL AND I STARTED WATCHING A SOAP OPERA.

It all started with Cheryl's mom. Every day at 3:00 in the afternoon, we could find her, a tablespoon of peanut butter in her hand, sitting in her chair watching her "soap." This was *her* time—time she took just for herself. I remember asking her why she had a tablespoon of peanut butter; she said that she loved peanut butter and if she spread it on something, that would be more calories, so she chose to eat it straight from the container and frankly, she liked it best that way.

Her "soap" was General Hospital. I remember when we started watching it with her. We happened to be passing through the cottage at the time General Hospital was on. We asked a couple of questions, watched for a few minutes, and went on with our day. The next couple of times we happened to pass through her cottage around 3:00, General Hospital was on again, so we asked some more questions and watched a little longer. Before we knew it, Cheryl and I were hooked.

From then on, each day at 3:00 p.m., we joined Cheryl's mom and watched the show with her. We even started grabbing a tablespoon of peanut butter and slowly eating it while we got caught up in the "drama" unfolding before our eyes.

The storyline included two characters named Luke and Laura who were involved in a complicated and convoluted love story full of secrets, suspense, mystery, and some murder or attempted murder. The story line captured the attention of viewers all around the United States. True to the soap opera genre, each day the storyline twisted and turned, building to a climax full of dramatic music and close-up camera shots on actors caught in deep, meaningful moments. The camera zoomed in on an actor's face, frozen with tension right after some heated dialogue. The actors stared at each other, holding the other's gaze as the music swelled; then, the show would be over for that day. Everyone watching the drama would hold their breath along with the actors, and let out an audible sigh when the theme music played and the credits rolled.

This tactic ensured that the audience came back the next day, getting caught up once again in the next part of the story. They even used this tactic when they went to commercial breaks, making sure they didn't lose their audience when the commercials would run. During commercials, Cheryl and I ran to the kitchen, grabbed more peanut butter and scurried back to our spots on the floor in front of the TV before the story resumed. The show started again, zooming out from the actors caught in their meaningful moment, and the action picked up once more.

It was quite a story! Pictures of Luke and Laura were on the covers of magazines and tabloids in every store. No matter where we went we overheard people discussing what they thought would happen next. And the storyline went on for YEARS. It's amazing how the writers of the show dragged out the story, giving audiences enough of a dopamine hit through each suspenseful swell that they were hooked and came back day after day, week after week, month after month, and year after year.

General Hospital was still a big hit when I was in high school. I worked at a nursing home, and many of the residents—the old folks—also watched the show! Around 3:00 p.m., the nurse's aides would meander into one of their rooms to check up on them and "visit." The show just happened to be on, and we got caught up in the story. Other aides wandered into the room and soon there were a bunch of us all watching another episode of General Hospital together. The old folks were just as into it as everyone else was!

That's the thing with soap operas: the constant "drama" hooks people in. They are drawn to the conflict, the arguments, the break ups, the new relationships, the mysterious strangers that come and go, and the never-ending turn of events. It's "drama" at its height! Plenty of reality shows streaming and on television today play on these tactics as well. Just think of the high drama of shows like *Keeping Up with the Kardashians* or *The Bachelor* and *The Bachelorette*—a new version of soap operas!

The funny thing is, watching the drama on soap operas reminds me a little of when I was in middle school. I remember the days and weeks of constant drama between friends: boys who liked one girl, then a different one; multiple girls who liked the same boy; boys who teased girls; the constant whispering back and forth of who likes whom and who doesn't like so and so anymore. There was drama between friends, drama in school, drama after school, drama in sports, drama, drama, drama!

Now with social media, this kind of drama can get out of hand. The drama is nonstop. The good thing about General Hospital was that we knew it lasted only an hour a day and that it was all fake. Yes, people thought about it and talked about it, but it was simply entertainment. These days social media drama, whatever the platform, can be never-ending if kids (and adults) don't learn how to keep it under control.

One of the most important things in middle school and in life is learning how to "handle the drama." Life can mirror a soap opera if we let it. But if we take captive our thoughts (as the Bible tells us to do in 2 Corinthians 10:5: "We take captive every thought to make it obedient to Christ") we'll be well on our way to living a "drama-free" life.

I have a rule with my high school drama students: "no drama in drama." We have work to do, and I expect them to leave their personal drama in the wings so we can focus on our real work of producing a great show. We have a lot of fun with our fabricated drama when our real-life drama gets taken out of the equation. It's a really good skill to learn and it serves us all well.

Taking our thoughts captive helps us stay focused on what's important. It can build wisdom and discernment as well. But how do we do that? Well, here are some suggestions:

1. If a friend has real drama going on in life, offer to pray for them. Share some inspirational quotes or scripture, or just be a good friend and give a listening ear.

2. Use something physical to help tame your thoughts. For example: Put on a stretchy bracelet that is easy to remove. Every time your thoughts wander to

something negative or "drama filled," take the bracelet off and switch it to the other wrist. When you put it on the other wrist, give your negative/drama-filled thoughts to God and ask Him to help you focus your mind on positive things. Each time you move the bracelet or wristband, also tell God something you are thankful for.

Today, I encourage you to leave the drama to the soap opera stars and go enjoy real life!!

 LEARN IT: 2 Corinthians 10:5

 DO IT:
- How often do your thoughts wander to something negative? What kind of drama is happening right now that tries to pull you in? What kind of strategies will you use to "take captive your thoughts"?

_____

_____

_____

_____

_____

28. BALANCE

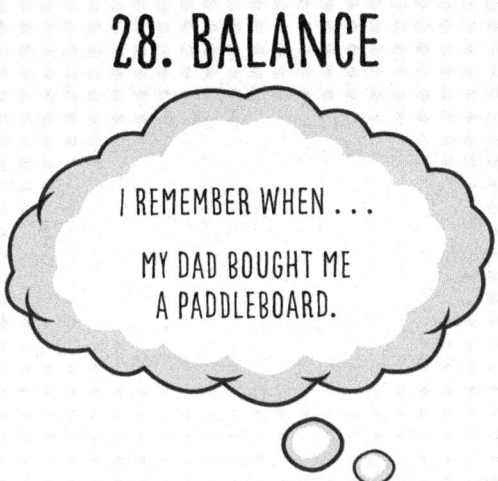

I REMEMBER WHEN . . .

MY DAD BOUGHT ME
A PADDLEBOARD.

I was already an adult, married and with kids of my own. One day when I was visiting the cottage with my kids, Cheryl came by on a paddleboard. She and her husband both had one, so she let me try hers, and I loved it! I think I borrowed it every day until one day, my dad returned from town with a paddleboard for me! (It was really a paddleboard for the cottage, but he bought it because of me, and I loved it.)

I went out on it every morning and paddled around the lake. It was quiet and still; a perfect way to enjoy nature, contemplate life and God's goodness, release any frustrations and struggles, give them to God, and soak in His beautiful creation surrounding me.

I also used the paddleboard for going out on the lake with others. I remember borrowing Cheryl's paddleboard so my daughter and I could go out together. One time, my childhood friend from Illinois also came, and the three of us went out on the boards. We were just paddling around when we decided to try some paddleboard yoga. My Illinois friend, Shirene, had seen it done in Florida, so of course we had to try it!

We each got on a paddleboard and tried some easy moves—up dog and down dog to be exact. We did these moves pretty well. Shirene tried some other moves, still fairly simple, and challenged me to try some as well. I liked yoga and had been doing quite a bit of it at home, so I tried some more challenging moves. I started easy again with a mountain pose and a sun salutation. When I got to lifting one leg up and raising my foot into the air, the board wobbled a bit and I lost my balance, toppling into the water with a big splash. My daughter laughed her head off, so I tried it again and challenged her to see if she could do any better. I'm happy to report that she couldn't!

It was a lot of fun trying and once I figured out the balance a little better, I could hold a pose for about three seconds before falling into the water again. It reminded me of all the times I tried things as a kid and fell into the water over and over and over.

Yoga is all about core strength and balance, and on a paddleboard, the balance part is even more important. When I do yoga in my living room, I just put my foot down and regain my balance. On a paddleboard however, when I started to tip, even if I tried to put my food down, the board wobbled and I fell in the water. It was fun to do, funny to watch, and because I love the water so much, I didn't mind falling in! However, it was hard to balance and do yoga on a paddleboard!

Balance is so important though. In middle school, there's a lot to balance: a bunch of different classes, different teachers, homework in different subjects, after-school activities, town sports, dance class, chores at home, church, youth group, personal devotions, family get-togethers and more. And somewhere in the midst of all that we have to eat and sleep. When I was in middle school, I had all those things as well, but I didn't have the internet, my own phone or computer, or social media. Add those things to the list and we may find ourselves falling into the water more than balancing on the paddleboard!

How can we learn to have balance in all the great things in life? It's a tricky question with a tricky answer. God has blessed us with so many good things, so how do we balance them all?

The Covid-19 pandemic helped a lot of people put things into perspective, including me. I am someone who likes to be busy and am involved in a lot of things. However, when everything shut down, I enjoyed being home, spending time with my family and not rushing off to all the various activities that had previously taken up so much of my time.

Balance is a bit like Sabbath. God created the world to be in balance. Whole books have been written about the delicate balance of creation and how small things can make huge changes! There are tons of documentaries and much research about the balance in nature. For instance, look up some articles and documentaries about bringing wolves back into Yellowstone National Park to restructure the predator/prey balance. It's fascinating!

But let's think back to yoga on a paddleboard and how that applies to balance in life.

First, it's challenging and takes work. When I'm on the board, I need to work hard at keeping my balance. In the same way, in my regular life I need to do the hard work at deciding what to say no to, even if those things are good, so I can say yes to better things. Colossians 3:2 is a good verse to have in mind to help us focus: "Set your minds on things above, not on earthly things."

Second, when I lose my balance on the paddleboard, I fall into the water. Similarly, when I lose balance in life, things start to fall apart. When I'm in the water, I can quickly jump back on the paddleboard and regain my balance, and the same thing applies to life. When we feel our lives get out of balance, we can do something about it. We can make decisions to get back into balance. Look at Psalm 118:13–14:

> "I was pushed back and about to fall, but the Lord helped me. The Lord is my strength and my defense; he has become my salvation."

I love this passage because it tells us that God is with us. He's there to help us stand.

Lastly (for now at least because this is a topic that needs a lot of attention in today's world), we need to make sure we have a Sabbath—a day, or at least a specific time, of rest. I don't mean sleeping (even though that is hugely important); I mean a specific time when we get away from all our activities. We need a time when we unplug from social media or other distractions online; a time when we put the homework, sports, dance, and other activities aside and spend time regaining balance.

I'm not talking about the Old Testament rules about not preparing food or walking a certain distance on the Sabbath. I'm also not talking about all the rules I had to follow on Sunday as a kid. I'm talking about the real Sabbath. There are a lot of scripture passages about the Sabbath, but when Jesus talks about it, He points away from the rules and regulations. Jesus is always about the heart. In Mark 2:27 He says, "The Sabbath was made for man, not man for the Sabbath." The bottom line is that God built Sabbath rest into the fabric of life. When we ignore rest and Sabbath, our lives get out of balance.

So today, friends, think about where you may need some balance. Do you need to unplug? Do you need to take a bike ride or do some paddleboard yoga? Do you need to sit and pray or journal your thoughts and give them to God? Whatever you need, take some time to regain your balance, to stop, think, pray, and take a deep breath.

Balance your life.

 LEARN IT: Mark 2:27

DO IT:

- Think through things that make you feel overwhelmed and then write them down. Often when we make a list of things, they tend to seem more manageable. We can also pinpoint areas in our lives that are causing stress. Sometimes those things can't go away, but we can learn to manage them by breaking things down and also by focusing on God's word and His promises. As you make your list, make another list full of ideas that can help you find balance and have Sabbath rest.

Things that make me feel overwhelmed:

Things that help me find balance and rest- Sabbath:

29. KICK THE CAN

I REMEMBER WHEN . . .
WE PLAYED "KICK THE CAN."

In the evenings, the parents got together and played cards at one of the cottages while the kids gathered in the yard.

The kids and parents from up on the hill came down to join the games too. We played all the way across the six yards on the landing. Our playing area was huge. The boundaries lengthwise ran from the farthest cottage on the right to the farthest cottage on the left. For depth, the boundaries ran from the road to the lake and out to the ends of the docks. Going inside the cottages was off limits but everything else was fair game.

The rules of the game were simple. One person was "it" and counted to a certain number while all the other kids hid. The kid who was "it" searched for the other kids, and when one was found, they raced to the can. If the person who was found kicked the can first, they were free to go hide again. But if the person who was "it" made it back to the can, the "found" person would be in jail and have to sit by the can as the game continued. As more people got caught, they hung out together by the can, waiting for that one super stealthy person who was able to kick the can and set them all free.

It was great! There were probably 10–20 kids of all ages playing. We played at dusk and wore dark clothes to blend into the background. We hid in trees, in boats, behind cottages, by sheds and garages. There were so many great places to hide!

I remember hiding in our speedboat with Cheryl. We climbed in and crouched down, swiping cobwebs out of the way. We crawled up front in the hull under the steering wheel and kept quiet. It was dark and we heard the faint sounds of crickets and bullfrogs in the distance as well as the mosquitos buzzing around our heads. We heard the hushed voices of the other kids who'd been found, chatting quietly as they sat around the "can" waiting for someone to come and kick it and deliver them. Then . . . as we whispered to each other, trying not to giggle and give ourselves away, we heard a twig snap, leaves rustle, and the muted sound of one set of feet pounding on the ground, sprinting toward the can. The voices at the can dropped to a low murmur of anticipation. Then, more muted pounding, another set of feet running, coming from a different direction . . . both sets racing to the can! We were silent, waiting…and then, that beautiful loud CLANK! as the can went flying, followed by the sounds of multiple feet scattering across the lawn as everyone looked for new hiding places. The person who was "it" picked up the can, placed it back in its circle, began counting again and the game continued.

I remember times when my hiding spot was so good that I wasn't found. Eventually I'd hear someone calling out,

"Allee, allee, all come free!" As a kid, I thought people were saying "allee, allee upcumfree." I never knew they were actual words, but I knew what it meant—everyone was to come out of hiding and gather around the can so we could start a new round.

The games went on for a long time—until it was pitch dark. There were bats and bugs, cobwebs and spiders, but I was never scared, I was excited! I always felt surrounded by everything good—family, friends, and fun. I remember the little bursts of adrenaline when someone snuck up and startled us. If that person was looking for a place to hide, we quickly pulled him or her into our hiding place with us. If that person was the one who was "it," we suddenly made a mad scramble and dash as we all raced to the can!

There's a section of Psalm 139 that reminds me of a big game of kick the can:

"Where can I go from your Spirit?
    Where can I flee from your presence?
If I go up to the heavens, you are there;
    if I make my bed in the depths, you are there.
If I rise on the wings of the dawn,
    if I settle on the far side of the sea,
even there your hand will guide me,
    your right hand will hold me fast.
If I say, "Surely the darkness will hide me
    and the light become night around me,"
even the darkness will not be dark to you;
    the night will shine like the day,
    for darkness is as light to you" (vv. 7–12).

This passage is similar to playing "hide and seek" or "kick the can" with God—but God is always "it" and He always wins. He finds us no matter where we hide.

Sometimes we try to hide from God like Adam and Eve did in Genesis 3. After they sinned, they knew they had done something wrong, so they tried to hide from God (good luck there!). Adam and Eve found they couldn't hide from God, but they tried, and sometimes we do that too. We may not be hiding like we would in a game of kick the can, but we may be consciously ignoring God's work in our lives. We may stop praying or attending church; we may avoid specific people or places that are good and positive influences in our lives and in doing so, avoid God as well.

At other times in life we may feel alone, like God just isn't around. Stressful things pile up and we wonder if God is real and if He really cares. But if we look at Psalm 139 again and really let it soak in (and even memorize it), we know that He is always with us. There is nowhere in all creation where we can get away from His presence!

This is a comforting thought as we go through life—especially during those times that are scary, stressful or just plain hard.

Just remember we are never alone, and we can't hide from God. He is always there. He always knows where we are and what we're going through. He will always "kick the can" and deliver us. There are many things in life that are filled with uncertainty, stress, and fear: pandemics, cancer, divorce—just to name a few. But God is in control. He knows about EVERY SINGLE THING. And He cares. He understands. He is with each one of us every single step of the way.

Today, let's rest in His promise and know that we are NEVER out of His sight.

 LEARN IT: Psalm 139:7–12

 DO IT:
- Write down some things that you may be trying to "hide" from God, and then realize that He knows them all anyways. Maybe you don't always "feel" God's presence, but write down ways in which you KNOW He is always with you. Look up promises that God makes in the Bible about His care and love for you. Write down these promises so you know them even when you may not feel them.

_____

_____

_____

_____

_____

_____

_____

30. PHONE CALLS AND BUSY SIGNALS

I REMEMBER WHEN . . .

OUR PHONES HAD PARTY LINES
OUT AT THE COTTAGE.

I had to be careful because back then, phones were very different than they are today. We had something called a "rotary dial" phone out at the cottage. It had a base and a handle attached to the phone by a long, curly cord. We had to pick up the handle to dial the phone and make a call. We held one end of the handle to an ear and spoke in the other. The entire thing attached to the wall by a different cord.

These phones didn't have any features beyond allowing incoming and outgoing calls. There was no "speed dial" or voice mail, and we didn't store our contacts in it. We had these big "phone books" sitting under the phone or in a drawer. The phone book had people's phone numbers listed in them alphabetically.

To dial, we'd pick up the handle and put it to our ear, then put a finger in the plastic circles corresponding to specific numbers on the dial. We had to rotate the dial once for every digit of the number we were calling. I remember when I got one of the single numbers wrong, or didn't bring the circle all the way around, I had to hang up the receiver, then pick it back up and start dialing the whole number all over again.

The phones at the cottage all connected to what a "party line." It wasn't a line for planning parties; rather, it was one phone line that multiple "parties," or families, used. Basically, all the cottages on either side of us, up and down the landing, shared the same phone line. We had different phone numbers, but one line.

So, when the phone rang, we had to listen for our specific ring pattern. It might have been one long ring and two short ones, or three short rings, or two long rings and a short one, but each cottage had its own pattern. If we didn't listen carefully and just picked up the phone, we may have answered our neighbor's call.

I remember picking up the phone and saying hello to some random person who asked for one of my neighbors. I realized the call wasn't for my family, apologized and asked them to call back. When they did, the phone in our cottage rang again, but I left it alone. Eventually the ringing stopped when the other neighbor answered it, or when the caller gave up. Sometimes I dialed a number and instead of a ring I'd hear a "buzz buzz buzz" pattern that meant the person I was trying to call was already on the phone and the line was "busy." There was no such thing as voice mail, so people couldn't leave messages. They simply had to call back later.

Being on a party line meant that you weren't always able to use the phone when you wanted to. There were times when I tried to call Cheryl; I picked up the phone and waited for the dial tone, but instead of hearing the dial tone, I heard another voice on the phone—it was one of my neighbors in a conversation with someone else! Even though we knew it might happen, it was always kind of surprising when it did!

Also, when we wanted to call someone who lived farther away, the phone companies charged us extra for making a "long distance" phone call. In fact, we got charged "long distance" just to call our friends across the lake!

Things sure have changed! Now we all have our own phones and we carry them with us everywhere we go. Phones are always accessible, and we can talk to our friends and families in a lot of different ways. Our phones aren't attached to a wall by a cord anymore—we carry them in our pockets or backpacks. Calling someone is easier than ever, even over long distances. There are rarely extra charges for calling someone out-of-state or across the country, which is good because cell service is pretty expensive as it is!

When I was growing up, people used to say that prayer was like making a phone call to God. They also liked to say that "if we called God, we'd never get a busy signal." It was just another way people tried to explain prayer.

The thing is, we can talk to God anytime, anywhere. We don't need a phone plan that costs a lot of money or the latest phone to do so. God is always available and will always listen. In fact, many passages tell us to "call" God! Jeremiah 33:1–3 says, "Call to me and I will answer you," and Psalm 17:6, Psalm 18:6, Psalm 30:2, Psalm 55:2, and Psalm 89:26 all talk about calling out to God and having Him hear and answer us.

Prayer is a fascinating thing; as often as people try to explain it, they fall short. That's why people try to simplify it and say it's like a phone call with God.

Today, as we use our phones to talk to family and friends, let's also take some time and talk to God. Have a conversation with Him. Tell Him all the fun things you are doing—as well as all the difficult things that may be happening. Tell Him your frustrations. Ask Him your questions. Share with Him your secrets—after all, He's the safest place for them, and He knows them already. He's always ready to listen, He LOVES it when we talk to Him, and He's never too busy!

Talk to Him today!

 LEARN IT: Jeremiah 33:1–3

 DO IT:

- Talk to God. It doesn't have to be a big, long prayer with all kinds of big words. Write down what you are thinking about and what questions you may have. Think of it like you're talking to a friend. You don't have to ask for things, just tell Him about your day. Tell Him anything about your life, your family, or really anything at all. Thank Him for all the great things in your life. Ask Him questions. Just have a nice chat. Give it a try!

31. TRULY AWESOME

I REMEMBER WHEN . . .
WE STARGAZED AT NIGHT.

In the middle of August, we went out late at night to watch the shooting stars during the Perseid meteor shower, which happens every year. It was one of my favorite times of the summer. Back then, people didn't have their houses lit up at night with outdoor sconces and spot lights like they do now. The cottages may have given off a soft glow of a light in a window here or there, but mainly, it was dark, which was perfect for stargazing.

I remember going outside with family or friends and gazing up at the sky. We saw so many stars and constellations! As I searched for the big dipper and the little dipper, I saw a flash of light streak across the sky. It was fast and the light went out quickly.

We stayed out for an hour or so, just looking up at the sky. I used to lay on the dock so I wouldn't get a crick in my neck. When I was in a chair on the shore, leaning back and looking up, my neck started to hurt from being in that position for too long. But when I laid on the dock, I could lie flat and look up at the inky sky, spattered with pinpricks of light. It was still and quiet, with only the occasional night noises of a fish jumping or a bug buzzing to break the silence. My family and I talked quietly while we watched the sky, and when we saw a shooting star, we pointed and asked in hushed tones, "Did you see that one?"

I loved looking at the sky and counting how many shooting stars we saw in one night. I still do it to this day. I love stargazing with my family—it's so cool when all of us see the same brilliant star blazing across the sky.

Shooting stars, or meteor showers, are fascinating. When I think of meteor showers, I am reminded of Psalm 8, especially verse 3 and following:

"When I consider your heavens,
    the work of your fingers,
the moon and the stars,
    which you have set in place,
what is mankind that you are mindful of them,
    human beings that you care for them?"

God is so amazing, so great, and so huge! Looking at the stars always makes me feel a bit closer to God, but also leaves me with a sense of awe and wonder as I realize how small I am in the midst of all creation. And not only all creation, but the whole expanse of time as well.

How can God, who is so massive, expansive, has been in existence forever, notice and pay any attention to me, this seemingly insignificant person who's currently living on earth for just a few years? God, the One who tracks each shooting star, who creates each molecule and grain of sand, who knows each atom and cell in every plant and animal—this God knows me and loves me . . . and you as well. When we stop and REALLY think about it, it is mind-boggling.

So today, try to put things into perspective. Look at the world around you. Stop what you're doing and take a moment to marvel at how amazing God's world is. The shooting stars are a good place to start. Even if it's not meteor shower season when you're reading this, still try to go outside at night and look at the stars. Find a spot where you can gaze up and see the magnificent sky and marvel at God's vastness. Think about Psalm 8 once again and meditate on verse 5, which talks about you and me:

> "You have made them a little lower than the angels and crowned them with glory and honor."

God, who made the stars, the universe, and everything in it, also made you and me. He crowned us as His children. He takes JOY in us! He delights in us! Just like parents delight in their kids, so also God delights in every one of us—but *even more* than our parents do. In fact, we'll never be able to comprehend how much God delights in us.

So, no matter what you may be feeling today, think about what you KNOW. Go outside tonight and look at the stars. Then think about or read Psalm 8 and let the words sink in. Let those words become part of the fabric of who you are, so that you know these truths and never doubt them.

We all have many questions, doubts, and fears. But there comes a point where we have to land somewhere. So today, land here, in the knowledge that God—the God who made the sun, the moon, every star and grain of sand, the entire universe—has crowned YOU as His child!

Be in awe, my friends.

 LEARN IT: Psalm 8

 DO IT:
- Look up the word "awe." What does it mean to be "in awe" of something or someone? What is something that inspires "awe" in you? Think about God, the creator of whatever that awe-inspiring thing is, and let your mind find even more awe and wonder in who God is. Then, know that this God, the creator of the universe, created and loves YOU!

_____

_____

_____

_____

_____

_____

_____

_____

_____

Made in USA - North Chelmsford, MA
1317721_9781625861887
06.10.2022 1504